This is the book all mothers need, no ma
wise, honest and healing, sensible and s

The Prayin

Every mother I've ever coached wonders about her effectiveness, questions her competence, and fears she's ruining her child for life. Jane reminds you that you are not alone on this journey, and she takes you by the hand in a comforting way. *Heartbeat of a Mother* answers the questions you're afraid to ask, offers the grace you desperately need, and offers you hope for a God-sized heart.

— SHANNON ETHRIDGE, life/relationship coach and author of *Every Woman's Battle Series*

Jane captures the heartbeat of every mom at every age or stage of life. She is compassionate and caring yet biblical and brave. Jane's writing is like having coffee with your wise best friend.

— PAM FARREL, author of *10 Best Decisions a Parent Can Make* and *Men Are Like Waffles—Women Are Like Spaghetti*

Every mother who's ever felt weary, guilty, or fearful will appreciate the wit and warmth poured into this six-week study. The wisdom in its pages will encourage her and bring reassurance that she's not alone. Thank you, Jane, for sharing your heart with other moms. We love you for it!

— GRACE FOX, international speaker and author of *Tuck-Me-In Talks with Your Little Ones*

Motherhood is wonderful, exhilarating, fantastic, and flat-out hard! *Heartbeat of a Mother* is like sitting down with a wise friend and receiving encouragement to thrive in the messy, imperfect craziness of motherhood. The readings are both short enough for the busiest mother to manage and meaningful enough to promote growth and healing for a mom's heart. This is a book for real mothers who parent real children.

— DE'ETTA GOECKER, homeschooling mom of nine, air force chaplain's wife, and served in leadership in PWOC, an international ministry to military women

I couldn't put this book down. It read like a cozy blanket wrapped around me. This is a book for real moms in every stage and season of life. The transparent readings will be a comfort and welcome friend. Throughout this insightful and relatable book, you are reminded that you are not alone.

— SUE HEIMER, international speaker and coauthor of *What I Wish I Had Known*

Heartbeat of a Mother is a not-to-be-missed book for every mom who has ever questioned her worth, second-guessed her parenting skills, worried over a child's wrong choices, longed to be a perfect parent, or desired to make a lasting impact on her child. This group study will strengthen your faith, validate your concerns, and give you a place to ask honest questions. Jane Rubietta has given us a tool for shedding shame and embracing grace in our roles as mothers!

— CAROL KENT, speaker and author of *When I Lay My Isaac Down*

With utter joy, I recommend *Heartbeat of a Mother* for every mama out there. Jane Rubietta's practical and poetical words take on the ups and downs of motherhood and will touch both your heart and mind. Devour this book, then share with a friend—your kids will thank you.

—LUCINDA SECREST MCDOWELL, author of *Dwelling Places*

Jane captures the pulse of a mother's heart and runs with it. With grace and ease, she unfolds the joy, pain, and pleasure of being fully alive and fully loved by God. Like a sweet dessert, her words will thrill your heart.

—GARI MEACHAM, author of *Spirit Hunger* and *Truly Fed*

My heart is full after reading *Heartbeat of a Mother*. Jane's words communicate biblical truth and godly wisdom. She addresses every season in the life of a mom with wit, understanding, and hope. I will enthusiastically recommend this book to the military moms I mentor and disciple!

—BRENDA PACE, veteran military wife, military ministry consultant, and coauthor of *Medals above My Heart: The Rewards of Being a Military Wife*

In her expressive, lyrical style, Jane Rubietta peels back layers of pretending to show the sometimes raw, sometimes aching, sometimes out-of-rhythm heartbeat of a mother. Speaking to women of all ages, not just the new mom but the seasoned, weary, or worried mom, Rubietta offers authentic, practical insights, a healthy dose of compassion, and poetic prayer pulses that steady and strengthen a mother's heartbeat. Moms will find affirmation and hope threaded through these pages.

—CYNTHIA RUCHTI, author of *Tattered and Mended: The Art of Healing the Wounded Soul*

Whether you live in the land of hope or regret, of wonder or bewilderment, Jane hears your heart in her newest book. A practical and beautiful tool for every mother's heart. Hold on. Healing and hope are on the way.

—JILL SAVAGE, CEO of Hearts at Home and author of *No More Perfect Moms*

"My mother's heart aches for you." I've said those words to many mothers as they've traveled through treacherous times with their children. My mother's heart has joined other moms in rejoicing and hoping, in gladness and song. *Heartbeat of a Mother* will walk with you through those moments and so many others. Thank you, Jane Rubietta, for your precious encouragement to mothers. Thanks for hearing our hearts beat.

—KENDRA SMILEY, speaker and author of *Journey of a Strong-Willed Child* and *Heart Clutter*

Heartbeat of a Mother

of a

Encouragement for the Lifelong Journey

To Emily!
God bless your
Mother Heart!

Jane Rubietta

With anticipation!

Jane Rubietta

Rom 5:5

wesleyan
PUBLISHING HOUSE
wphstore.com

Library of Congress Cataloging-in-Publication Data

Rubietta, Jane, author.
Heartbeat of a mother : encouragement for the lifelong journey / Jane Rubietta.
Indianapolis : Wesleyan Publishing House, 2016.
LCCN 2015047731 I ISBN 9781632571502 (pbk.)
LCSH: Motherhood--Religious aspects--Christianity. I
    Mothers--Religious life.
LCC BV4529.18 .R83 2016 I DDC 248.8/431--dc23 LC record available at
http://lccn.loc.gov/2015047731

Names and identifying details have been changed to protect the privacy of individuals.

Cover design: Cody Rayn

To mothers everywhere, all doing the best they can, hoping against hope for the very best for their children.

To my mother, whose love is always with me.

To my children, who stole my heart and who teach me daily about real love.

Contents

Free shepherding resources are available at
wphresources.com/heartbeat.

Introduction

My baby's heartbeat pounded steadily, a taut cadence of hope as the doctor placed the cold stethoscope on my tummy. Joy and wonder shivered through my heart. What a miracle! What a privilege! What a launch into the unknown. Who could imagine that this helpless, endearing infant would instantly steal my heart only to return it, years later (say, at adolescence) bruised and battered like a demolition derby car?

I entered the mothering season with high hopes, with, as a song from *Les Misérables* puts it, "a heart full of love." But before I could say "oxytocin," I realized how quickly that heart of love is depleted in the wake of exhaustion, colicky babies, and the twenty-four-hour responsibilities of parenting. How do we live with a heart full of love in light of the drain and strain on this feeble, fickle instrument?

As a child, I acquired a perfect little plastic family from Fisher-Price, complete with a never-rumpled plastic sofa, two small plastic children, and a plastic puppy that never grew up or threw up. Something was wrong with that picture. Families aren't molded to perfection. They are composed of willful human beings—people who make mistakes, get exhausted, and run out of words and patience amid the frustrating stream of interruptions flowing from the very people they are trying to love. Crazily, even the most loving moms end up at cross-purposes with themselves.

So let's pack away the pretend people with their always-happy families, the parents who are unfailingly patient and kind, the ever-obedient dog, and the furniture that is never soiled by an overflowing diaper or spilled juice box or a sloppy busy teenager or a ricocheting or missing adult child.

Heartbeat of a Mother is for real mothers with messy hearts and homes. For women who love their children—and sometimes can't stand them. In thirty-six readings, we take an honest, balanced look at mothers' hearts—their dreams, fears, mistakes, and heartbreaks. We talk about the laughter and tears, mountains and deserts, endorphins and antidepressants, hope and despair. This is for the mothers who have questioned how such wild pendulum swings can occupy the same heart, who have wondered why other mothers don't feel this way. The truth is, they do.

Heartbeat of a Mother is a book for the hearts of mothers who aren't perfect and whose children aren't perfect. For mothers of all ages who carry, packed in their hearts, both delights and regrets, whose maternal scrapbook contains both memories and mistakes. This is for women who need to know they are not alone, they are loved, and there is help for every heartache.

Each entry of the six-part soul book centers around a familiar heart expression and builds on a scriptural principle and an anecdote or illustration. Each day begins either with a real-life story from my own experience or with one of the thousands of mother stories I hear each year. A Heart Verse opens each chapter and offers a heart full of hope, encouragement, wisdom, and perspective from God's Word. Use it for meditation or just for breathing in God's presence. The Heart Work section invites you into the spiritual discipline of rest or silence in order to allow God to work in your heart at a deeper level. This moment is critical to the inner work of the Holy Spirit and to the healing of our hearts so essential to parenting well. Next, the Heart Check section poses soul-deepening questions that invite us into greater wholeness. These are ideal questions for journaling or for small group facilitation. The Heart Cry section delivers a poignant prayer, expressing thoughts drawn from the reading and application sections, a prayer written almost as poetry. Try reading these words aloud.

We deeply long to hear God's voice. Thus, a benediction titled Heart of God closes each reading. These are words God might whisper or sing over us. Sometimes we need to hear them over and over, so take your time and soak in the blessing.

Hope

Part 1

While I don't seek a career majoring on numbers, I do love them. I love to quantify, to crunch numbers so a bottom line or percentage or ratio appears. Amid the vast unknowns of life, numbers provide solid information, which helps me feel a bit safer.

Numbers offer the security of knowing. With numbers, I understand situations and possibilities better. Numbers tell me what choices to make. Take gas prices, for instance. That dollar amount, factored with the number of gallons left in the tank, tells me whether to buy now or hold out for a better deal. Whether it's the reading on a bathroom scale, the balance on a bank account, the results on lab reports, or the marks on a yardstick, numbers put facts at our fingertips so we can make informed decisions. (Interpretation: Numbers clue me in as to whether or not I should worry.)

The thing about hope is that you can't quantify it, measure it, or calculate numbers to arrive at it. The certainty of hope—there's an oxymoron if ever there was one—is like faith, the assurance of things hoped for, the conviction of things not seen (see Heb. 11:1). Hope is the opposite of numbers, which arrive at certainty by quantifying, classifying, and categorizing. Maybe that's why I find it so hard to hope: I want to rely on results I can see and measure, on objective results.

We can categorize and measure a great deal: a child's birth time and date or a baby's length and weight. Statisticians tell us, based on census figures, that it will cost about a quarter of a million dollars to raise a child born in 2013, or upwards of three hundred thousand dollars after adjusting for inflation and including public education through college.[1] Does that include the cost of defiance? Our own or our children's? The cost of deferred or destroyed dreams, of destructive relationships? The cost of a broken heart?

Who can deny the difficulty and costs of motherhood—the ups, the downs, the spin-arounds, the "I don't know," the "How do I . . . ?" and the "But I thought . . ." all of which leave us feeling a little more helpless and, sometimes, honestly, a little low on the lumens of hope. Numbers don't lie, but they don't always add up either—not to hope. Figures and finances seem unrelated to, even the opposite of, hope. At least, I hope that's true.

So when we feel like our hope fund is depleted, what do we do? As mothers, we can't crunch numbers when it comes to hope— for ourselves, our children, or our world. Moms can't afford to rely on numbers, stats, or a calculator display that represents our lives or the lives of our children. Or the sum of our life experiences. Some investment offers and even medications come with a warning: Past performance is not a guarantee of future results. We can't afford to have our hope for the future, our hope for our children, based on the past—unless we're looking at how God has operated in the past.

Hope is patience with the lamp lit.

—TERTULLIAN

We can categorize God's character and likely responses because we have seen God at work. So if faith is the assurance of things hoped for, the conviction of things not seen (see Heb. 11:1), what if we look backward at the things we *have* seen? They may not be directly related to our hopes for our children or to the facts and figures that currently represent their lives. But the things we have seen point to God's love for us, God's steadfast, never-failing love. The Hebrew term for that is *hesed*. That kind of love we can take to the bank. It sure sounds like hope to me. This same God of never-failing love holds our children's hands, and that adds up to a bottom line we can count on.

"For I know the plans that I have for you,"
declares the LORD, "plans for welfare and not for
calamity to give you a future and a hope."

—JEREMIAH 29:11 NASB

The apostle Paul, who knew all about misplaced hopes, offered this prayer: "May the God of hope fill you with all joy and peace as you trust in him, so that you may overflow with hope by the power of the Holy Spirit" (Rom. 15:13). The reality we have is not what we see but, rather, the God of hope, who fills us with hope as we trust that his past performance is a guarantee of future results. So we overflow with hope. Hope then becomes buoyant, having a resilience that refuses to be destroyed. And hope grows, swelling into an offering to others. As a long-ago prayer reads, "Where there is despair, let me sow hope."[2] And that defies all the odds, all the number crunching, all the adding and subtracting of our daily lives. Today, we receive and we sow hope.

Notes

1. Emily Thomas, "This Is How Much It Costs to Raise a Child in the US," *The Huffington Post*, last updated September 2, 2014, http://www.huffingtonpost.com/2014/08/18/cost-of-raising-a-child_n_5688179.html.

2. Although widely attributed to St. Francis, this quote originated from *La Clochette* (The Little Bell) (*La Ligue de la Sainte-Messe* [The League of the Holy Mass], 1912). *Wikipedia*, s.v. "Prayer of Saint Francis," last modified January 17, 2016, https://en.wikipedia.org/wiki/Prayer_of_Saint_Francis.

I will give thanks to the LORD with all my heart;
I will tell of all Your wonders.

—Psalm 9:1 NASB

1

With All My Heart

I never really thought about my heart, the blood it pumped through my long body, the work it performed ceaselessly all day and all night. I did notice with appreciation that elevated blood pressure from exercise translated into the burning of calories, and I welcomed the flushed face and pounding beat. Otherwise, I don't ever remember thinking, "Wow, I'm so glad my heart is beating." It just does.

*"During an average lifetime, the heart will pump
nearly 1.5 million barrels of blood—enough
to fill two hundred train tank cars."*[1]

How aware I became of my heartbeat when my babies came to rest in the nest below this hardworking organ. It seemed as though the quantity of blood in my circulatory system doubled from the normal four to six quarts in an adult body. (Think about that, though:

six quarts is one and a half gallons of blood. That seems like quite a bit of liquid sloshing through our systems.) I noticed my pulse pushing against my throat, neck, chest, wrists, temples. I could literally *hear* my heartbeat and feel it pressing clear to the edge of my fingertips. All of my heart responded to this new body occupation: gestating a baby.

Heart rate may increase up to 15 percent during pregnancy. Blood volume increases progressively . . . creating a need for increased iron and folic acid intake.[2]

Then my focus changed. When the doctor pressed that icy stethoscope against my bulging belly and let me listen, I heard not my own heartbeat but the quick cadence of this unborn child's heart. I didn't realize then that my children would forever be representative of my heart—they would always be just a beat, a thought, a pulse away, even after birth. Though I carried them no longer, my heart fled my body with their birth and followed them.

Whether adopted or birthed from our womb, whether bottle- or breast-fed, these babies carry our hearts with them, like well-hidden stowaways, for the rest of their—no, our own—lives. Our hearts travel the world, trailing stealthily after our kids through their first wobbly steps around a table, their first trundling toddle from one set of arms to another, their first trip to school, their first fight with a friend, their first love, and their first heartbreak. A mother's heart should qualify for a frequent flyer program, logging millions of miles pounding after her children.

*Every day the heart creates enough energy to
drive a truck twenty miles. In a lifetime, that is
equivalent to driving to the moon and back.*[3]

No matter their ages right now, no matter our age, this very minute as mothers our hearts beat after our children. Whether they live in California or Connecticut, attend college or sleep in a cradle, wear diapers or designer jeans, are twenty inches long or six feet tall, these children become the default setting on our brain's operating system and our heart's monitor. Even as we go about our days, working in- and outside the home, settling labor disputes or sibling disagreements, filling multiple roles, sometimes on autopilot and sometimes at high levels of concentration, there, secure in a teeny though perhaps unconscious spot in our heart, rest our children.

Who knew? Before becoming mothers, we couldn't possibly have known the joy and the journey toward wholeness these babies would bring. (A nice way of saying children bring out the worst in us so we can begin to get well.) We couldn't have known how hard it would be to see them wobble off on their own and return sobbing. We had no idea, fortunately, of the cost of being mothers, of externalizing our heart and letting it crawl, then walk, then run around in small but growing bodies, moving progressively farther away from us.

My closest friends have children living overseas, across the country, across town, in their own homes, and in a bassinet in their bedroom. And like million-mile strands of yarn attached to their heels, our thoughts follow these children. Our hearts latch on to them, beat for them, pray for them, weep with them, and laugh with them. We hope; we love; we agonize.

Before becoming a mother, when I heard the phrase "with all my heart," I took it as a term used to demonstrate sincerity. Now, with my three children in various stages of growing up and out and away, "with all my heart" means they have all of me, the very essence of me, the part of me that keeps me alive.

But that is not entirely accurate, is it? While our thoughts may tag after them like a tail on a kite and our hearts move in their direction, we are very much limited in our capacity to be with our children. But that is not the end of the story either, as we stand on the stoop and wave them off on the bus, on a first solo bike ride, on their first date, to a school dance, to a first job, down the aisle, or across the country. For with all our hearts, we can turn these precious, externalized heartbeats over to the One who said, "I am with you always, even to the end of the age" (Matt. 28:20 NASB). Thankfully, we can trust with all our hearts the One who keeps our hearts beating keeps their hearts beating as well.

Heart Work

With all your heart, stop and pull your children to your mind: the worries, the joys, the fear, the goodness, the sadness. Now imagine putting each child (no matter how big!) one at a time on Jesus' lap. Tell him what worries you, like you'd tell a babysitter: "Tommy has nightmares, and this is how I handle it." But Jesus is no babysitter. He is with them always and has even more of a heart for them than you do.

Give your child to Jesus with all your heart. Invite him to hold your heart as well. Wait there and practice giving thanks with all your heart: for yourself (yes, even though you might feel awkward or self-centered), for God's work in you, for God's work through you, and for God's work for your children.

Heart Check

What does "with all my heart" mean to you? When do you use that phrase? And what does the sentiment encapsulate?

At what times do you feel that you and your kids were cheated because your heart didn't have much capacity for loving? Periods when your heart didn't offer much of a reservoir from which to love? What do you do in those empty-reservoir times?

What do you hope for, with all your heart, for yourself? It's OK and good to verbalize these things. How can we recognize God's guidance us if we don't know our own heart? And what do you hope for, with all your heart, for your loved ones?

Heart Cry

Sometimes I forget
That I can ask for more of a heart,
So that "with all my heart"
Becomes a bigger and better blessing
Because my heart has grown.
Help me, God,
To love fully
Out of the fullness of your love,
So that "with all my heart"
Means an unlimited bounty of goodness.
And for all the times
When I cannot be near my children,
The heart of my heart,
You are.
And you have even more of a heart than I.
Thank you for loving them,
For loving me,
With all your heart.

Heart of God

Dear one,
With all my heart
I send hope
And help to you
Through my Son
And the Holy Spirit
Pouring into your heart.
When you are empty,
I have more.
When you are desolate,
My heart is full.
When you are hope-deprived,
Come to me.
I will fill you with my love,
With my hope.
Wherever you wobble or wander,
Wherever your children wobble or wander,
I will find you
And fill you
Because I love you
With all my heart.

Notes

1. "36 Interesting Facts About . . . The Human Heart," Random history.com, posted January 28, 2010, http://facts.randomhistory.com/human-heart-facts.html.

2. "What Bodily Changes Can You Expect During Pregnancy?" Healthline, last updated June 4, 2012, http://www.healthline.com/health/pregnancy/bodily-changes-during#CirculatorySystemChanges4.

3. "36 Interesting Facts."

So those who went off with heavy hearts will come
home laughing, with armloads of blessing.

—Psalm 126:6 MSG

2

Bless Your Heart

Growing up in the South, I heard the words "Bless your heart"
a hundred times a day, always spoken with gentle, sympathetic,
tones by women with cheeks softer than a powder puff and
smoother than the skin of a newborn. Just say, "Bless your heart,"
and memories swirl of sweet tea and throaty laughter and bright
summer sun.

I love this phrase, but when overused it becomes meaningless
and trite. "Bless your heart" disintegrates into a catchphrase, a soft
murmuring sound uttered when other words make no sense or don't
appear. Just three meaningless filler words. Even worse, spoken with
just the right inflection, "Bless her heart" becomes a putdown, a *tsk-
tsk* equivalent to "What a shame." With just the teeniest dose of low
self-worth, we could hear those familiar words as "You are to be
pitied" or "You are in trouble" or "You are a failure."

Isn't this easy for mothers to believe? Don't we internalize our
children's mishaps, failures, and shortcomings, figuring that if our

young ones don't grow up to be decent people with good jobs it is likely our fault? We've all heard that behind every great person stands a self-sacrificing, saintly mother. So the opposite must be true as well. If good children have good mothers, then children who stray or are less than perfect or don't fit into the triumphant Christmas letter must have bad mothers. We believe this, even if we don't verbalize it or put it into writing. When our children misbehave, we *tut-tut* ourselves and spike the blame meter in our own hearts.

Then we play the "if only" game. If only I had been more available, and more present. If only I had smiled more and yelled less. If only I hadn't worked outside the home or had homeschooled the children; or if only I *had* worked outside the home or put the children in private schools. If only I had detected that problem sooner and remortgaged the house to get the help my child needed.

We need to stop that ranting of our sore heart. What if we reclaim this blessing? As a woman, I desperately want my heart to be blessed. As a mother, more than almost anything, I want my children's hearts to be blessed.

Listen to David's words: "I cry out, GOD, call out: 'You're my last chance, my only hope for life!' Oh listen, please listen; I've never been this low. Rescue me from those who are hunting me down; I'm no match for them. Get me out of this dungeon so I can thank you in public. Your people will form a circle around me and you'll bring me showers of blessing!" (Ps. 142:6–7 MSG). David understood the difficulty of living in uncertainty, poverty, and the drought of being without blessing.

*Give freely and spontaneously. Don't have a
stingy heart. The way you handle matters like this
triggers GOD, your God's, blessing in everything
you do, all your work and ventures.*

—DEUTERONOMY 15:10 MSG

So what does "bless your heart" really mean? To bless means to invoke divine care of or to confer prosperity or happiness upon. It means to consecrate, sanctify, or approve. What better to pray over our hearts than a true blessing!

*The LORD said to Moses, "Tell Aaron and his sons, 'This is
how you are to bless the Israelites. Say to them: "The LORD
bless you and keep you; the LORD make his face shine on
you and be gracious to you; the LORD turn his face toward
you and give you peace."' So they will put my name
on the Israelites, and I will bless them."*

—NUMBERS 6:22–27

For every single day you have been a parent, I pray, "God, bless her heart." Bless your heart, my friend. Every step you took, nose you wiped, bed you made, lunch you prepared, meal you balanced, green veggie you force-fed. Bless your heart for every tantrum you deflected, bruise you kissed, back you rubbed. For every time you felt like a failure, a mistake, a mismatch in the parent-child dance, bless your heart. For every time you've *tut-tutted* yourself, felt shame for your actions, cried for your children, bless your heart.

Just listen one more time: Bless your heart.

Heart Work

If no one else says a bless-your-heart prayer over you, you can do it yourself. Try this: Put your hand over your heart. Feel through your palm the lub-dub, lub-dub that faithful beating you so often take for granted. Listen and breathe. "God, bless my heart. Thank you for this instrument that so reflects my life, my situation, my loves. Bless my heart. Help it to beat in rhythm with your heart. Confer your divine care over this instrument, both the physical organ and the seat of my emotions."

And after you've asked God to bless your own heart, do the same with your children. If they are still young enough to welcome your touch, place your hand over their hearts and bless them. "God, bless this heart. Keep it pure, happy, focused, and healthy." If your baby birds flew the coop (or are prickly teens), raise your hand toward heaven and bless their hearts long distance.

Heart Check

What do the words "bless your heart" mean to you? Who in your life has ever said those words to you? Who has said it as though invoking a divine blessing, and who has said it as a *tsk-tsking*?

In what instances do you hear this triplet of words as a shaming phrase when you could just as easily hear it as a blessing? Why do you do that? How could you change your interpretation?

What happened within you when you placed your hand over your own heart and asked God to bless it (that is, to consecrate it and confer a blessing, hope, peace, prosperity, and happiness)? Take back the power of this phrase and use it often: over yourself, your children, your own mother (or mother-in-law), and other women you meet: "Bless your heart."

Heart Cry

Bless *my* heart?
Is that even OK?
I'm so busy
Trying to confer blessing
On others—
On the small- and large-footed people
In my life—
That I forget about my own heart
And how desperate I am for
You to bless it, God.
Bless my heart, God.
Let me hear your words over me,
Your longing for me,
Your gracious offering of peace,
Of happiness,
Of hope.
Set aside my heart
For you.
And bless my heart
That I might bless others' hearts too.

Heart of God

Dear one,
Your questions and efforts,
Your agonies and joys,
Your uncertainties and hopes,
Your doubts and dreams,
Your misgivings and givings,
Your poverty and richness
Have not gone unnoticed or ignored.
I heard,
I still hear,
And I say over you,
Thank you
And
Bless your heart.

Sometimes it's hard for you to hear me,
So listen up.
Press your ear to my heart
And hear it again:
Bless
Your
Heart.
I mean it
With all my heart.

Search me, O God, and know my heart; try me and know
my anxious thoughts; and see if there be any hurtful way
in me, and lead me in the everlasting way.

—Psalm 139:23–24 NASB

3

Heart Inspection

The women's ministry coordinator threw lollipops at her should-be-napping children and called me during what was meant to be her free time. How she managed to oversee the women's ministry at her huge church while raising three children baffled me, but I was delighted to be part of her church's women's retreat.

"We'd like something in the area of spiritual disciplines," she said.

I groaned internally and waited, listening, knowing from a former pastor that every staff member and volunteer at her church had been inundated with teaching on the disciplines over the past ten years. My silence allowed her time to elaborate.

"What I mean is, we're all so tired. We just want to catch our breath."

Ah. That's what I wanted to hear. "How about if we work with the promise, 'Catch your breath. Find your heart.' Because more than anything, women's exhaustion has cost them their heart."

Her voice choked up at the other end of the phone line.

She is no different from you or me. Our responsibilities spawn enormous to-do lists and tremendous exhaustion, and it shows up in our hearts. It's hard to laugh, hard to cry, and easier to keep running, to stop feeling.

But then we die. At least, we die emotionally. But the good news, and our source of ginormous confidence as well: Where there's life, there's hope.

Imagine this: You are at the doctor's office, and your physician looks you in the eyes and asks, "How's your heart?"

The average adult heart beats seventy-two times a minute; a hundred thousand times a day; 3.6 million times a year; and 2.5 billion times during a lifetime.[1]

First, how does it feel to be asked that question? And what do you say in response? You know the doctor doesn't mean, "Is your heart still beating?" Presumably it is, since you are upright and breathing. No, the physician wants to know how your heart feels. What's your immediate response to the doctor's question? The tip-of-tongue answer, without forethought or people-pleasing. Is it a shoulder shrug, a stoic half grin, an "All is well"? Is it, "Just fine, good, great, thank you"? Or maybe you raise your brow slightly, meaning, "You're kidding me."

It's not as though we don't know where our heart is; it's beating right beneath our sternum. But the stress on our heart from days or weeks or years or decades of being a mother and a woman in this wild world leaves us more than a little winded. In the marathon of mothering, we can tend to only a handful of problems at a time. Usually others' problems occupy the available heart time. During the heavy mothering years, those are primarily our children's needs and problems: whether normal aches and pains, a painful early-childhood diagnosis, a call from the principal or the ER, a married child in crisis, or a prodigal trying to escape the reach of your heart.

A kitchen faucet would need to be turned on all the way for at least forty-five years to equal the amount of blood pumped by the heart in an average lifetime.[2]

But this question is not about our children for a change. This is our time for a long overdue checkup on the state of our hearts, a time of inspection. Stop and wait in silence for a few minutes—or as long as it takes for the noise of your list-filled life to subside. Ask God to let you feel your heart, the rhythms and arrhythmias, the lubs and dubs. Then breathe in a great big dose of hope. It's just what the doctor ordered.

Heart Work

Flatten your palm against your sternum. Don't do anything else. Just get comfortable and sit still with your hand flat against your chest. Wait, noticing how your heartbeat responds to your thoughts. Sometimes anxious thoughts produce quicker beats. What is your heart telling you about yourself? Your lifestyle?

Heart Check

Who gets the giant's portion of your heart's attention? Whose problems or what issues occupy your heart space?

What is your immediate response to the doctor's question: "How's your heart?"

Wait with the question and listen. How is your heart, really? What underlying message is it beating out for you in some mysterious Morse code, hoping you will notice and respond appropriately?

Heart Cry

Lord, is it too good to be true?
How I long to catch my breath,
To find and feel my heart again.
My heart thuds beneath my breastbone,
Anxious to be heard, honored, cared for.
No one else can do this for me,
So I drag my bedraggled soul to you.
I breathe in.
I breathe out.
And listen.

Heart of God

Dear one,
I can hear
Your heartbeat
And listen
Even when you are silent,
Even when you have no words,
Even when you do not know
Your own heart.
I hear
And I love
And I heal.
Pay attention to the Morse code
Of your soul,
And let me help interpret.
Your heart is talking to you;
Let's listen together.
I am your personal
Great Physician.

Notes

1. "36 Interesting Facts About . . . The Human Heart," Random history.com, posted January 28, 2010, http://facts.randomhistory.com/ human-heart-facts.html.
2. Ibid.

A cheerful heart is good medicine.
—Proverbs 17:22

4
The Merry Heart

When my brother, who is thirteen months older than I am, had an idea when we were children, it was always good, and I'd follow him like a devoted puppy. No doubt he loved this. One day when we were in fifth and sixth grades, we decided it might be important to see if we could climb out of the ground-level bathroom window. You never know when such knowledge could be useful. Any number of potential careers might call for this level of experience.

So we shoved the awning window out as far as it would open, and John stood on the toilet then squeezed himself through the opening. I held his legs until his long, lean body bent in half over the window frame. His legs followed his torso, and he caught himself with his hands in the dirt underneath the window.

My turn. Though shorter than John, I still managed to maneuver my bony, thin, uncoordinated body through the window. I rested on the frame, half in, half out, like some poor gymnast trying to balance on her stomach but folding in two like a newspaper. When that pose became painful, I scraped the rest of my skin-and-bones self over the wood casing and plunged to the ground.

That was fun. So much so that we decided to climb back in the house through the window.

At that unfortunate moment, our neighbor happened to peer between the bushes separating our lawns. A stereotypical nosy old lady, she spotted the "burglars" climbing through the window. Ever helpful, she alerted the police, who arrived at the scene of the crime at about the same time my parents pulled up the driveway.

When the "helpful" neighbor relayed the details to the police and my mother, John and I materialized as the burglars. My mother hooted. As my mom's huge laughter carried over the yard to the street, effectively sounding an all-clear, the neighbor slunk away. The police closed their notepads, shooting a grimace at the neighbor's retreating back. With merry eyes, Mom laughed until her cheeks flushed.

Health experts now have proof that laughter is good medicine. A good belly laugh can send 20 percent more blood flowing through your entire body. One study found that when people watched a funny movie, their blood flow increased. That's why laughter might just be the perfect antidote to stress.[1]

My mother never took serious problems lightly, but no one had a better funny bone than she did. Even now, with grown grandchildren and suffering from chronic pain, she breaks out in a laugh regularly, and many times we have laughed until we couldn't talk. We have doubled over from laughter on Saturday nights watching the antics of *The Carol Burnett Show* or the early years of *Saturday Night Live*. When hard times arrive—and they do for every family—shared laughter creates a lovely bond. In the midst of difficult times, a good laugh offers hope that the ultimate reality is far different from what current problems imply.

Laughing changes my perspective. And my heart. Authorities say that people who laugh, last.

Laughter can decrease stress hormones, reduce artery inflammation and increase HDL, the "good" cholesterol.

—Dr. Suzanne Steinbaum, cardiologist[2]

After I became a parent, too often I lost the struggle to keep a sense of humor amid the exhaustion and turmoil of mothering. Remembering my mother's model always helps. She still says, "I kept telling myself, if I could just get you grown before I died of laughter or, at least, make it to the next room before bursting, it would be a miracle."

And we survived a childhood fraught with "criminal" potential, so I guess it was just that—a miracle.

Heart Work

Sometimes I think Jesus just throws back his head and laughs at us. We take ourselves and our window-climbing expeditions so seriously, but we are meant to be children at heart, exploring our limits and the limits of the world around us. Wait with your heart and listen. See if you can get Jesus' perspective. Can you hear him laugh? It will be worth the wait. And while you're at it, ask God for a merry heart. God loves to share the fun.

Heart Check

Recall a time as a child when you needed to hear laughter and instead heard chastising. What was the laughter level in your home?

How about now: What tickles your funny bone? When was the last time you held your sides in laughter or your stomach muscles hurt the next day because of a laugh-fest? What was so funny? How does laughter affect your heart?

Who in your life helps you laugh and helps restore your perspective? How often do you get together? Get a date on your calendar or start keeping watch for a funny-bone friend. If you can figure out how to laugh or at least smile, it will change your heart's condition. It's good medicine.

Heart Cry

Oh, Jesus!
I want to hear your laughter
Instead of always expecting
Disapproval or judgment from you.
I can't wait until I see
You face-to-face and
See your perspective,
Find your funny bone,
Watch the tears run down your cheeks
As you tell stories about us growing up
This side of heaven.
You will swing me up into your arms
And plop me on your lap
And laugh with me.
Until then,
Help me to laugh more
And to last;
Because a merry heart
Does this body good.

Heart of God

Dear one,
I love your antics.
I love to hear your laugh.
Laughter takes faith,
And it requires perspective,
And I have enough to go around.
I see the beginning from the end
And all points in between.
So go ahead.
Belly laughs are good for the soul
And the heart
And your relationships;
And laughter brings a light heart.
It sounds a lot like
Hope.

Notes

1. Stephanie Watson, "Amazing Facts about Heart Health and Heart Disease," WebMD, reviewed July 2, 2009, http://www.webmd.com/heart/features/amazing-facts-about-heart-health-and-heart-disease_?page=2.
2. "Humor Helps Your Heart? How?" American Heart Association, last updated June 24, 2015, http://www.heart.org/HEART ORG/Getting Healthy/Humor-helps-your-heart-How_UCM_447039_ Article.jsp.

Since this is the kind of life we have chosen, the life of the Spirit, let us make sure that we . . . work out its implications in every detail of our lives. That means we will not compare ourselves with each other as if one of us were better and another worse. We have far more interesting things to do with our lives. Each of us is an original.

—Galatians 5:25–26 MSG

5

The Compassionate Heart

When I walked into her home, I skidded to a stop, my heart hammering with appreciation—and a little bit more. Smooth kitchen counters, refurbished antiques, and warm arrangements of furniture graced her house. No toys littered the floor, and no dust ate its way into the finish of the furniture. We could have staged an impromptu photo shoot without rearranging or hiding a single item. I wanted to be like my friend.

Another friend homeschools her children. Her endless reserves of patience and laughter contribute to making happy, healthy kids. This woman owns the mother gene in enormous quantities. I wanted to be like her too.

A third friend is hugely boisterous, with a big laugh and an ocean-sized heart. A hundred creative projects pile about her home. She is cutting-edge, brilliant, and deep. She sews, knits, embroiders, and teaches her kids to paint and think creatively. She reads voraciously and is generous with her time and talents. I wanted to be like her.

A fourth friend juggles a high-paying profession with a blended family and steady volunteering at her local church. Her keen intellect and penchant for organization combine with a high emotional quotient, making her serene. I wanted to be like her.

A heart at peace gives life to the body,
but envy rots the bones.

—Proverbs 14:30

I see women with different gifts and graces everywhere. Meanwhile, my detriments pile up to make a load of insufficiency. I don't want to be me, sometimes, because me isn't good enough. *Me* isn't like *her*. My brain doesn't function like hers. I'm certain my family will wake up on the floor some morning because the dust mites have gnawed our beds out from under us. Though our meals are nutritious and seldom from a box, our kids likely ingested significant quantities of preservatives and a bit of hydrogenated oil during the hurry-up years of early childhood. Sheer survival is one of the great wonders of the world, in our home anyway.

Strength lies in differences, not in similarities.

—Stephen R. Covey[1]

Always, we moms see our own need for improvement. Other mothers do life and family better or neater or happier than we do. Our human nature makes us watch others and wonder why they are different and thus better.

*History records a 100 percent absence of perfect
parents. Even Adam and Eve failed, and they had
a perfect parent—God. Plus, they never had
to live through their own teenage years.*

Our kids will pay some price for living in our homes, no matter
how smart or creative or organized or inexhaustible we are. But
consider the coins you've thrown into the tollbooths of your own
life in order to arrive at this junction today. Life is costly; wounds
and inadequacies are real. The journey is ours alone, shaping us and
influencing our families. We can't escape this.

It starts right here, in our messy or clean homes with our organized or cluttered minds and our grip on God's hand in this journey
toward holiness. We can't change our pasts, but we can work with
God to become the best versions of ourselves we can be. We'll be
different from one another, but different is inevitable. And different
is good.

And our children? One day, they'll join the refrain: "My past is
mine alone. I can't change it. But I can become myself." So we all
get the same choice. Welcome to hope.

Heart Work

Is it possible that you are exactly the mother your children need?
Why else would God have given you to each other? Wait with that
question on your heart, and invite God to speak into your current situation, into your past, and into your fears and regrets and comparisons
with other moms who seem (or seemed) to do this so much better
than you. Just wait, letting your heart stabilize and letting God bring
you to a place of rest and acceptance.

Heart Check

Who is the ideal mother in your eyes, the woman you always compare yourself to and then judge yourself lacking? What mother envy rises in your heart? Where do you feel inadequate when you see other moms?

Compassion for others, including our own children, begins with compassion for ourselves and the journey we've taken. What parts of your journey have shaped you into the woman you are today, the mother you're becoming? How can you begin to appreciate those mile markers?

Think of your journey as one leading to holiness. Where do you see evidence of that in your life? What difference does that thought make when you are tempted to compare yourself to others?

Heart Cry

Whoa, God!
If you examine my heart—
And you do!—
I'm certain you see
How I compare myself to others
And always fall short.
Yet you have clearly called
Me into this profession of woman and mother,
So here I am.
All my failings,
My inadequacies.
I am less than I expected,
Less than my friends in so many ways.
But you have given me a child
To raise and nurture,
And you knew what kind
Of a deal you were giving the child:
Me,
A broken woman
With messes inside and out.

But you know me,
You call me,
You love me,
And your Holy Spirit enables me
To love and grow
In the gifts and graces.
So here I am.
Bowed before you,
Grateful I am not alone,
And neither is my child.

Heart of God

Dear one,
I still shake my head in wonder
Over you,
Over your one-of-a-kind-ness.
And I think,
"Nice. Good job. Heavenly high fives."
You are you
And designed for a purpose
With gifts and graces only you can offer.
So stop comparing.
You have every reason for hope.
You measure up in my sight.
And wonder of wonders,
You will never stop growing
Into the woman
You're created to be,
An original, one-of-a-kind
You.

Note

1. "Quotes About Community," Goodreads.com, accessed February 24, 2016, http://www.goodreads.com/quotes/tag/community.

GOD made my life complete when I placed all the pieces before him. When I cleaned up my act, he gave me a fresh start. Indeed, I've kept alert to GOD's ways; I haven't taken God for granted. Every day I review the ways he works, I try not to miss a trick. I feel put back together, and I'm watching my step. GOD rewrote the text of my life when I opened the book of my heart to his eyes.

—2 Samuel 22:21–25 MSG

6

Restart Your Heart

We look at our children. We look back on our years of parenting, many years for some of us, years that unfurled like a red carpet or unraveled like the loose end on a sweater. Perhaps time has given us perspective. This would be a kindness. But too often when our kids smack into obstacles like billiard balls on a pool table, regrets consume us. Self-doubt begins its shaming and finger pointing, announcing to our sad hearts that perhaps things would have turned out better if only . . .

If only we had homeschooled the children like so-and-so with her perfect kids or hadn't homeschooled at all or instead spent the money on a Christian school.

If only we had refinanced our house to save that kid from addiction or if only we hadn't.

If only we had earned more money or saved more money or quit that job or hadn't worked so many hours.

If only we had paid closer attention or listened more and yelled less.

If only we hadn't worried about a clean house before friends came over.

If only we hadn't been a single mom.

If only we had sought counseling for ourselves or for our child or for the whole family.

If only we had created a safer environment or better boundaries.

If only we worried less and smiled more.

If only we had more faith in the hard times or been wiser or more courageous.

If only we hadn't been so strict or had been stricter or loved more and disciplined less or disciplined more and loved . . . less?

If only we hadn't said those words or had kept the communication lines open.

If only we had taken more risks.

If only we had been firmer or given more freedom.

If only we had been more positive or focused on the good or shown more grace.

If only we had played more or laughed more.

If only we prayed more.

"If only" is an endless list, always written past tense. And we can't change the past. But we have hope, because God doesn't live in the past. God lives in the present, and the past is, well, past. All we can do is live right now and try to jump-start our hearts out of the dead-battery stage of "if only."

Regrets from yesterday delay living today.
Replay, pray, release. Repeat as needed.

Regrets and "if only" lists are useless. They are stall tactics preventing us from moving forward. God has good plans for our hearts, if we can jump-start them. All we can do is work on our own heart today. And pray for the hearts of our children.

Heart Work

"If only" equals regret. Wait with your general sense of "if only," letting specific instances of regret rise to the surface. Invite God to make his presence known to you as you review those images. Ask God to help you start over, to forgive you, and to restart your heart today. A restart equals hope.

Heart Check

Create your own "if only list." Write it out by hand, taking the time to experience the emotions that lie behind the "if only" litany. What happens within you as you write your list? As you view your list?

What can you change about how you are present today in your own heart?

Restarting your heart takes practice. Every time you find yourself filled with regret today, ask God to help you notice and to give you a new start. Confess anything necessary so you can start with a clean slate.

Heart Cry

Dear God,
I need a jump-start
On the battery of my heart.
Help me to notice my own
"If onlys" and the ones I think
I see in the eyes of people I love.

Restart my heart with the
Gift of forgiveness.
Help me to live today
In your presence,
In the present tense,
And learn to live
Without regret.
Because right now
Is all we get.

Heart of God

Dear one,
The litany of "if only"
Will take away your hope
And force your gaze always
Behind you.
But look to me.
Look me in the eyes.
See the love I have for you.
I don't want you to miss today
Because of yesterday.
Hand your list to me.
Lay it on the altar.
Burn it in the campfire.
Watch it go up in smoke,
And then
Let's start a new list called
Today.
Repeat after me:
"Today I will watch.
Today I will love.
Today I will really see the hope.
Today I will know I am loved."
With your new litany,
Others will know
They are loved too.
Just like you.

Rest

Part 2

There is no tired quite like mother tired. The circles under the eyes, the slow recovery from raising a newborn. Slogging through day after day, so much to do, so little sleep. We love, love, love our children. And we are so, so, so tired.

That fatigue isn't limited to newborn days and "I outgrew my nap" afternoons. On many long nights, a teenager sat at the computer while I stretched out on the floor as we conversed about a poem's meaning for the paper due the next morning. As my children grew, so did my calling to include writing and speaking. My nights shortened even as my children's responsibilities and waking hours lengthened.

I loved every minute of those days and nights—except for the pressing fatigue. Oh, and the impact of fatigue on my brain cells and body function.

In Psalm 127:3, we read, "Don't you see that children are G OD's best gift?" (MSG). On many days, or most days—or maybe every single day for some mothers—we would agree. Children are God's best and most amazing gift.

But just a line earlier, the wise psalmist's words are rendered, "Don't you know [God] enjoys giving rest to those he loves?" (Ps. 127:2 MSG). So, presumably, the gift of children and the gift of rest are not mutually exclusive.

That's such a lovely thought, but the majority of us do not find that overlapping section on the Venn diagram of our life, the one that combines rest and children. In fact, a survey taken in 2006 shows that of five hundred mothers, 54 percent reported not sleeping enough, and 59 percent were working full time. Half of the working mothers said they slept six or fewer hours a night. Of the stay-at-home moms, 48 percent said they were sleep deficient.[1] I can only imagine that these numbers are more extreme today.

If the heart has a resting rate, I wonder how many of us experience it? Sometimes, after I climb the steps to the bedroom, or even when I simply lie down on the floor of my office for a catnap, my heart thunders beneath my sternum as though protesting the shift from standing and working to resting. It pounds about in my chest like a bass drummer learning some fancy new rhythm.

A friend advises—and indeed, experts recommend and CEOs of major companies endorse—taking a twenty-minute nap if we start to feel drowsy, setting an alarm to awaken us and turning off our gadgets that make noise. Any longer than twenty minutes and we move into a different quality sleep that makes it harder to reboot our bodies. But that power nap can work wonders for our creativity and energy levels, not to mention our interpersonal skills—all compromised by fatigue.

*In vain you rise early and stay up late, toiling for food
to eat—for he grants sleep to those he loves.*

—Psalm 127:2

Most heart attacks occur on Monday mornings.[2] Surely that's a
result of soul exhaustion and dread. Whatever our age, our bodies
and souls speak loud and clear: Give us rest from our labors, rest
from our worries, and rest from our doubts, questions, and fears.

Vast amounts of medical research support the need for sleep, the
negative effects of sleep deprivation, and the benefits of sleep.
Beyond all that data, sleep feels good. Our bodies cry out for rest.

And so do our souls.

Exhaustion is not the mark of a faith-filled woman. Sometimes
my ability to function with little sleep becomes a boasting point,
sort of a "look at how amazing I am, I can sleep four hours and still
be here with you and get a long list of to-dos checked off" badge of
valor. It's not something I'm proud of because, more likely, my lack
of sleep points to my lack of faith. Logging too few hours of sleep
indicates my inability to trust that God is truly God, the creator and
sustainer of the universe, God the Son who upholds the entire world
by his powerful word (see Heb. 1:3).

Sleep is more than a necessity for our children. Maybe we could
speak or sing this old Welsh folk song over our own souls:

> Sleep my child and peace attend thee,
> All through the night.
> Guardian angels God will send thee,
> All through the night.
> Soft the drowsy hours are creeping,

Hill and vale in slumber steeping,
I my loving vigil keeping,
All through the night.

While the moon her watch is keeping,
All through the night.
While the weary world is sleeping,
All through the night.
O'er thy spirit gently stealing,
Visions of delight revealing,
Breathes a pure and holy feeling,
All through the night.[3]

All through the night. Sounds like heavenly peace. Can we put rest on our must-do list? It may be the most supreme act of faith we attempt.

Notes

1. "Yawn! Most Mothers Don't Get Enough Sleep," NBCNews, last updated October 20, 2006, http://www.nbcnews.com/ id/15347691/ns/ health-sleep/t/yawn-most-mothers-dont-get-enough-sleep/#.Vfww9NJ Vikp.

2. Stephanie Watson, "Amazing Facts about Heart Health and Heart Disease," WebMD, reviewed July 2, 2009, http://www.webmd.com/ heart/features/amazing-facts-about-heart-health-and-heart-disease_? page=2.

3. John Ceiriog Hughes, "Ar Hud y Nos" (All through the Night), trans. Harold Boulton, 1884, public domain.

I remain confident of this: I will see the goodness of the LORD
in the land of the living. Wait for the LORD; be strong
and take heart and wait for the LORD.

—Psalm 27:13–14

1

The Weary Heart

Outside the wind whips leaves from trees and they tumble down into the yard. This scene looks like my house every Thursday when I leave for speaking events: a whirlwind or dumping out my luggage contents, pouring out all the papers in my briefcase, sorting file folders and flight envelopes into piles, then reloading all with the upcoming event's requirements.

My son just called from college and filled in some blanks on his life: classes, midterms, work schedule, and an exciting upcoming project. Then he stopped and asked, "Wait. This feels like the Me Show. How are you, Mom?"

It does my heart good to have him ask. But before I could professionally mother-ize my answer, the words escaped: "I'm so tired." I almost burst into tears, the weariness sweeping over me so quickly that it swept me off my mother-guard, a leaf torn from the tree. I felt the fatigue in my chest—not just figuratively, but literally in my heart. Speaking has taken me all over the country this season, with lovely opportunities to be part of God's work around the nation. But I'm averaging only two and a half days at home per week. That's not enough time to keep the home fires burning, love my husband well, and tend to administrative work in my home office—let alone sleep.

Animals deprived entirely of sleep lose all immune function and die in just a matter of weeks. This is further supported by findings that many of the major restorative functions in the body like muscle growth, tissue repair, protein synthesis, and growth hormone release occur mostly, or in some cases only, during sleep.[1]

Women work seven days a week, even without a paycheck job. What a toll living must take on our hearts. And that's just what we notice from the outside. Inside, without our help, the heart works nonstop from its very first beat in our mother's womb until the last beat before we cross over to heaven. That's more than 2.5 million beats in a lifetime.

No wonder we get tired.

After my son's question, a friend's note arrived in the mail. With remarkable God-timing, she included a little Scripture card that bore the invitation, "Come to me, all you who are weary." Tears again gathered in my eyes, and I clutched the Scripture and leaned my head back against the chair. My weary heart spilled over, and I felt like I was spilling out all over the carpet. I actually opened my eyes, checking to see if I was springing leaks. All I could say was, "I'm so tired, Jesus. I'm so tired."

Sleep now, O sleep now,
O you unquiet heart!
A voice crying "Sleep now"
Is heard in my heart.

—James Joyce[2]

Though it was past noon and I'd been awake for seven hours, I hadn't yet made my daily list. Even so, I didn't jump up for my neon yellow cardstock (easier to find in my piles of papers) to start the process.

No, I sat in my chair, my heart tipping over into the room like water from a broken pitcher. And I pleaded, "God, help. I'm so tired. I can't do this." With fatigue comes discouragement, and I wondered how I'd outpaced my life so drastically. I considered bailing on tomorrow's all-day meeting. I thought maybe I'd quit being a writer.

But sitting there in the middle of the family room while the wind roared like Dorothy's tornado threatening to swoosh me off to Oz, I still didn't move away from Jesus. I waited, pouring out my heart.

And somehow, as I waited with my worn little heart spilling all over Jesus, strength rose within me. After maybe fifteen minutes, I stood up, made my list, and set it down. When I returned to the neon cardstock two hours later, I crossed off every single item.

Magic? No. Just Jesus, doing what he promised in Matthew 11:28, "Come to me, all you who are weary and burdened, and I will give you rest."

Heart Work

How about your heart today? Find your favorite chair or sofa or scrunch up your pillow on your bed and just be still with your soul. Breathe deeply and keep waiting. Let your heart catch up with your body. Keep waiting and don't start a list. Just ask, gently, "Where am I tired?" It might not be a physical fatigue but rather an emotional or even spiritual tiredness. When you begin to sense where you are weary, let it spill over onto Jesus. Spring leaks until the weariness seeps out and Christ sinks in. Then wait, rest, and repeat as needed.

Heart Check

Where is the whirlwind in your life? When do you most notice it?

When you wait with your heart, what is the first tired place that shows up? The second?

How much of Psalm 27:13–14 do you believe? How much do you experience? How can you begin to experience the goodness of the Lord in the land of the living and "take heart"?

Heart Cry

Dear God,
My heart tumbles against my chest
Like the leaves outside,
Like the thoughts in my head.
And I feel the weariness
As it spills over me,
Out of me.
Catch me, Jesus.
Catch my vitals
Pouring out of this leaking vessel,
And restore me
To your rest,

To your life.
Thank you
That I don't have to mother-ize
My response.
Thank you
That you can handle
My heart.

Heart of God

Dear one,
Sometimes being strong
And taking heart
Looks like rest,
Taking a load off
By trusting me
To care for you.
It's what I do.
Can you trust me today
With your exhaustion,
With your too-long list,
With your too-little energy?
Together we will accomplish
Just what needs to happen for today.
And tomorrow?
Tomorrow is another chance
For me to show
How much I love you.

Notes

1. "Why Do We Sleep, Anyway?" Division of Sleep Medicine at Harvard Medical School, last reviewd December 18, 2007, http://healthysleep.med.harvard.edu/healthy/matters/benefits-of-sleep/why-do-we-sleep.
2. James Joyce, "Sleep Now, O Sleep Now," PoemHunter.com, http://www.poemhunter.com/poems/sleep/page-1/33389/.

Hear me, you who know what is right, you people who have
taken my instruction to heart: Do not fear the reproach of [others]
or be terrified by their insults. . . . My righteousness will
last forever, my salvation through all generations.

—Isaiah 51:7–8

8

On Your Heart

We met on a military base, and she stood in line with two books
clutched against her rib cage. "You made me laugh, and you made
me cry," she said.

"Really? Cry? At what point did you feel tears?" Tears, I think,
are often—or even usually—indicative of the work of the Holy
Spirit on softening hearts.

She couldn't remember right then but returned five minutes later
with an answer. She said, "I wanted to tell you. When my baby was
born and I was exhausted, I just needed to sleep. My mother-in-law
came to visit and told me, 'I can count on one hand the number of
naps I took as a mother of five children.'"

This brave military wife interpreted those words as an instruction
manual for parenting. The law of mothering went something like this:
Push through your pain and keep going, look busy, be productive,
achieve, accomplish, activate. Anything else is unacceptable.

*When we are sleep deprived, our focus, attention, and
vigilance drift, making it more difficult to receive information.
Without adequate rest, over-worked neurons can no longer
function to coordinate information properly, and we lose
our ability to access previously learned information.*[1]

"Her words turned me into the kind of woman I never wanted to
be. I became overactive, involved, hurried, and never had time for
my children. Always pushing." Taking care of her own needs wasn't
an option. This was not a multiple-choice test. If she listened to her
husband's mother, only one way, one plan, existed to measure up.
And so she worked and ran and lost her heart amid the harried life
she created, never realizing the cost. Her regrets piled up.

The night we met, she determined to live differently, conscious
of her own heart and needs. She chose to start functioning out of
God's fullness rather than her own emptiness.

What a life-giving choice. Surely the Holy Spirit puts on our
hearts a longing for God, a desire to be completed by God's infill-
ing and not our own efforts. Hebrews 10:16 tells us, "I'm writing
out the plan *in* them, carving it on the lining of their hearts" (MSG).
This mother realized the toll her style of parenting exacted on her
heart—and on her children. Super-involvement that comes from
living under another's laws elevates our stress levels, which con-
tributes to the possibility of heart disease. A diseased heart will not
work, not well and not for long.

*In the United States, one in four women dies from
heart disease. In fact, coronary heart disease—the most
common type of heart disease—is the number one
killer of both men and women in the United States.*[2]

So we learn, in time, to listen to the words written on our hearts,
to the longings that come standard issue. We can begin to honor
those God-given desires for the joy of relationship, the pleasure of
being productive, the privilege of trusting God for times of rest and
replenishment. These are the lines carved on our hearts.

When we listen to the wrong voices, we confer an unwitting cost
on our children. So no matter our kids' ages, we slowly learn to trust
that God will carve a path with them too, writing out that plan on
their hearts' lining. Even now God plans to reverse that cost as we
heal, help them heal, and help them listen to God's voice.

My new friend left our meeting eager to run the race before her,
relieved that the true longing of her heart was inscribed in God's
handwriting.

Heart Work

Reread Hebrews 10:16 and let it seep into your heart and soul.
Put aside thoughts of productivity and achievements. Breathe in
the grace found in God's words written in your heart. Rest in this
truth: God's righteousness and salvation last forever, through all
generations.

Heart Check

Whose voice is inscribed in your heart when it comes to your rules for being a mother? What are some of those rules, and where did they originate?

What toll has your perhaps-unwitting code of motherhood taken on your heart? On your children? On your husband? On other significant relationships?

The Scriptures invite us who have God's words in our hearts not to be terrified by the way others judge us (for example, 1 Tim. 4:12). In what practical ways can you move closer to God and listen less to the voices prescribing insanity for you and, consequently, for your family?

Heart Cry

Dear God,
Always around me
I see women who do
This parenting job
Better or easier or neater or wiser
Than I seem to.
Their voices drown me
And drown out
Your voice, your love, your righteousness.
Help me to hear
The words you've written
On my heart
And to trust you
For my own heart
And for the lives of my children
Down through all generations.

Heart of God

Dear one,
You have no idea the weight
Other women carry
Trying to keep their own rules
Or another's rules for them
As they mother their own children.
Today is a good time
To list the rules you've inherited,
Rules you've written yourself,
Rules to live by,
Rules that define a good mother.
And then, bring those rules to me.
Let me rewrite them to include
My own personalized best for you.
It looks like resting from your labor.
It looks like resting from your attempts
To measure up or win favor
From another—or from me.
It looks like
Being free from the rule keeping
And turning to me.
I created you
For rest,
For trust,
For grace,
And you can trust me.
I have enough for you.
I love you.
And that should give you
Rest
For your soul.

Notes

1. "Sleep, Learning, and Memory," Division of Sleep Medicine at Harvard Medical School, last reviewed December 18, 2007, http://healthysleep.med.harvard.edu/healthy/matters/benefits-of-sleep/learning-memory.

2. "How Does Heart Disease Affect Women?" National Heart, Lung, and Blood Institute, last updated April 21, 2014, http://www.nhlbi.nih.gov/health/health-topics/ topics/hdw.

You have put gladness in my heart, more than when their grain
and new wine abound. In peace I will both lie down and sleep,
for You alone, O LORD, make me to dwell in safety.

—Psalm 4:7–8 NASB

9

Heart Fatigue

Question: When is a mom not busy?

Answer: When she's sleeping.

Except that's not true. (It's also not funny.) Sleep time is a busy time. There are so many people in the middle of a mother's night—babies crying, small children padding into the room rubbing nightmares from their eyes, teenagers knocking on the bedroom door just shy of curfew to say, "I'm home." And for the rest of their lives, mothers stash a phone by the bed in case the dreaded middle-of-the-night call ever comes. When does a mom ever sleep through the night?

A psychology major told me that awakening a patient every couple of hours can induce psychosis. Maybe that's one problem with mothering: We are all psychotic because we don't get enough sleep! I'm kidding of course, but don't miss the point. Moms are busy, so busy that we sometimes don't know which voices to listen to or what reality is—and, come to think of it, those are both symptoms of psychosis.

Sleep plays a critical role in brain development in infants and young children. Infants spend about thirteen to fourteen hours per day sleeping, about half of that time is spent in REM sleep, the stage in which most dreams occur. A link between sleep and brain plasticity is becoming clear in adults as well [evidenced by] the effect [of] sleep deprivation . . . on people's ability to learn and perform a variety of tasks.[1]

Fatigue skews our perceptions and leaves us off-balance. We make poor decisions, love poorly, and react poorly to problems and conflicts. Lack of sleep or poor sleep is linked to arterial aging and increased risk of heart attack. The neurotransmitters that help suppress pain don't recover, so we feel more physical pain. Our bodies simply don't heal well without enough sleep. And too little shut-eye destroys our souls and our relationships and leaves a wake of despair.

Where does this leave us? With chronic heart fatigue.

This is unacceptable. We can't afford to live this way.

Of course there are sleep disorders, physical or psychological conditions that affect our ability to get a good night's rest and mess with our energy levels.[2] And we're so busy during the day that we don't take time to process what we've experienced, so all that turmoil shows up at bedtime. Plus, mothers rarely sleep through the night until their kids go to college. For the rest of our lives, mothers have that nagging thought that their children need mothering, no matter how old they are.

How do we turn over the reins of responsibility and let someone else be in charge for seven hours at a stretch so we can sleep?

Do you remember the children's prayer, "Now I lay me down to sleep. I pray the Lord my soul to keep"? We have a soul-keeper, Jesus, the Good Shepherd, who longs to restore our souls and have us lie down in green pastures—or in beds with pillows and comforters.

To sleep, ultimately, means trusting God enough to relinquish agendas, ours and others', into God's good and capable care. God is bigger than our fears and our what-if questions, bigger than our guilt and shame, bigger than the messy house and piles of laundry and all other un-dones in our lives.

And trust, like sleep, is good for the heart.

Heart Work

Take some deep breaths and let your heart do its work. Wait in the stillness, listening to your heartbeat, listening to your heart fatigue. Where is your exhaustion? Turn that turmoil into prayer. When each weary thought appears, say, "God, hear my prayers." If it comes back, breathe again and say, "God, hear my prayers." God will hear and give rest. Wait and let rest seep into your soul.

Heart Check

Who wakes you in the night, either by their physical presence or by arousing a subconscious concern within you?

At what times do you find yourself most exhausted? Which of the symptoms of lack of sleep do you experience? When was the last time you talked with your doctor about fatigue and lack of sleep?

Where does your faith come into play in your physical practices of rest? What green pastures is the Good Shepherd inviting you to rest in? How and when will you say yes?

Heart Cry

Dear Good, Good Shepherd,
Now I lay me down to sleep.
Rather, I wish I could sleep,
But there's much to do to
Earn my keep.
I'm so tired I want to weep.
Would you hold me till my eyelids droop
And rest my mind and body too?
Let me sleep this night in peace
And wake tomorrow in your keep.

Heart of God

Dear one,
What if tonight
You crawl into bed
And pray this prayer:
"Now I lay me down to sleep.
My Shepherd holds me in his keep.
I count far more than sheep.
In his arms in peace I will lie down and sleep."
I will keep you
And the world
While you rest.

Notes

1. "Why Do We Sleep, Anyway?" Division of Sleep Medicine at Harvard Medical School, last updated December 18, 2007, http://healthysleep.med.harvard.edu/healthy/matters/benefits-of-sleep/why-do-we-sleep.
2. If you think you have a sleep disorder, talk with your doctor. This book is not intended to minimize in any way the importance of seeking medical attention for your heart and all things that disrupt it.

I will give them a heart to know me, that I am the LORD.
They will be my people, and I will be their God,
for they will return to me with all their heart.

—Jeremiah 24:7

10
A Heart to Know God

In a roomful of women, I ask about their mother hearts. What hurts their hearts? An astounding number of mothers pull me aside to whisper, "My child has left the faith." These moms raised their children in the hope of Scripture but lived with the unfortunate reality of mother-and-father failures, fathers who abandon, children's friends with a magnetic pull, addictions that promise endless excitement, or a world that wounds them.

These mothers blame themselves, living for years with a litany of "sooners." "If I'd gotten help sooner." "If I'd left their alcoholic father sooner." "I should have noticed sooner." This lament, chanted by moms around the world, tears into their hearts like studded tires on concrete. They wonder how to live with the regret. Their sorrows multiplied as their children veered off the narrow way onto rutted roads and wrong turns, landing them in a self-imposed exile from God. They have kids in prison, in dead-end jobs, having kids, on welfare, on the street, with eating disorders, divorced, depressed. They have kids living far from the starry-eyed hopes of the mothers who cradled them as newborns, fresh from God and full of potential.

Not a single one of these mothers expected her child to grow up to a life of crime or pain or desperate searching and disillusionment. These moms watched as their babies grew and developed their own wills, choosing their own next steps. Where once the mothers picked out the perfect shoes and held tiny wrists to help their children learn to walk, those mothers had to release their holds and allow their children to wander off through thistles and rock piles and dead ends.

Nothing can shake me; he's right by my side.
I'm glad from the inside out, ecstatic;
I've pitched my tent in the land of hope.

—ACTS 2:25–26 MSG

But the mothers in that group, despite their tears and breaking hearts, refuse to believe their children will not return. They walk about in brokenness but also in hope. One mom, once a prodigal herself and now the mother of a worrisome teen, texted me with a joke: "Did you hear about the prodigal who shook his fist and yelled, 'Leave me alone, God!'? God said, 'I can't. Your mom won't leave *me* alone!'"

I want to weep at the power of hope, weep for the prayers of mothers the world over, who barrage heaven constantly that their children may find God's heart again or for the first time. For God to bring those babies back from exile. Until the second they die, mothers carry their children in their heart, and day after day they hold the truth—Jesus' words—tight to their aching chests: "In this world you will have trouble. But take heart! I have overcome the world" (John 16:33). Jesus has overcome the world, and that counts for us and for our children. We can rest our weary souls—hearts sore from banging about in our cage of helplessness—in Christ's competence and ultimate triumph.

Cry. Wait. Hope.

—PSALM 130, CONDENSED AND PARAPHRASED

With that hope in their hearts, these mothers can release their children once again, along with their own demands about how their children's return to the fold will look. They whisper in wobbling voices, as though on a bicycle ridden over a washboard, "Whatever it takes, God. Whatever it takes." And they trust this faithful Savior to bring their children back to God's heart.

Heart Work

Bring your heart into a quiet place. Wait with your soul so full of longing and fear, regret and hope. In the stillness, offer those conflicting emotions to God. As you wait, ask God to remind you of the truth of his Word, his love, and his leading.

Heart Check

Recall the moment your child was first placed on your chest or in your arms. What hopes rose within you? What emotions? What fears? What certainties?

If your child is one of the lost hearts, what "sooner" litany do you recite? What do you do when you feel regret? If you are seeking God on behalf of a friend's child, how can you help that friend sound out her hopes and regrets?

How has your child's wandering affected your own relationship with God? What enables you to find hope amid your child's exile?

Heart Cry

All I ever wanted
Was for my baby to grow up
With a heart of faith
And knowing your love.
Look how it's turned out.
My heart aches
And my rib cage tightens
In grief's grip.
I choose to look to your truth
To you who said
"I will never leave you."
And even though a child
Seems to have left your side,
You haven't moved.
Please appear.
Please show yourself to this lonely exile.
Make yourself visible
On this dusty back-road detour to faith.
Come alongside.
Love my child
Back to your heart.
And I choose, today,
To release my regrets and my grip.
I refuse to live in exile,
Though I have certainly failed,
Leaving boulders of regret in the pathway
And obstacles for my child to overcome.
I refuse to turn away from you
Or from hope for my child.
Because you promised.

Heart of God

Dear one,
It's too soon to quit hoping,
Too soon to quit praying,
Too soon to quit growing.
But now is a good time
To relinquish your regrets and your fears.
Go ahead;
List them all,
Then wad them into a ball
And throw them away.
Heave them at heaven
And then do the math:
My longing for your child to return
Is a million times bigger
Than your own.
It's too soon to quit hoping.
Rest in this truth:
I will give your child
A heart to know me.

He tends his flock like a shepherd: He gathers the lambs
in his arms and carries them close to his heart;
he gently leads those that have young.

—Isaiah 40:11

11

Close to His Heart

How unforgettable, the days of having children. Even now,
twenty years since my youngest child's birth, eighteen years since
our little lambs nursed, I remember—who could forget?—the
painful engorgement, the swelling, the physical tenderness, the
exhaustion, the roller-coaster ride of joy and depletion. Does every
mother feel the certainty of inadequacy, never sure of the right next
step to take and the isolation that accompanies that ignorance not
wanting to ask too many questions or appear incompetent?

*High levels of stress hormones are strongly
linked to clinical depression.*[1]

Aren't we supposed to know this, to intuit this mothering business?
Our bodies sure seem to get it—increasing the liquid in our systems,
pouring the right hormones through us, ramping up the circulation.

But I didn't know, so I kept quiet about the questions and the mood swings, even when the black clouds settled over my soul, parking like a year-long summer storm.

Whether a child is birthed from our wombs or from our hearts, motherhood is not without its moments of despair. And this most magnificent profession and calling is not without a rescue from that darkness. Isaiah tells us that God "gently leads those that have young" (Isa. 40:11). Imagine the ewes, swollen and tender from birthing their lambs and so far from the greening fields of sustenance. How arduous must be that trek to recovery, and how long the journey for a ewe nursing her lamb. But the shepherd knows when to rest them and when to move them along the path.

Savior, like a shepherd lead us, much we need thy tender care;
In thy pleasant pastures feed us, for our use thy folds prepare.

—DOROTHY A. THRUPP[2]

God knows that mothers tend to outrun the Shepherd's gentle leadership and bypass the resting places along the way. Do we expect more of ourselves than God expects of us? God knows both our limits and the Shepherd's capabilities. God knows how vital it is for mothers to recover, get strong, and keep feeding their babies while the Shepherd feeds the mamas.

What about those wee kids, so young and awkward and willful and needy, so vulnerable to enemies, so like our own children with their bleating cries for comfort and food. How frightening to set them free from their resting place beneath our hearts, where they were protected from the outside world.

But the Shepherd cares for the babies too. He "gathers the lambs in his arms and carries them close to his heart" (Isa. 40:11). This comforts me, even now, with my children grown. Especially now. They will always be my lambs, but they are also Christ's. Even in their most stubborn places, they are weak and hurting; their disobedience, willful behavior, or slowness—all a result of their own hearts—cries for comfort, food, and safety. Jesus knows. He gathers them and tucks them in his arms and close to his heart.

When our babies lived in the womb, our own pulse steadily filled them with all they needed. That regular lub-dubbing brought comfort and nourishment and consistency. And now, though they may be far from us and can no longer hear our hearts steadying them, they are close to God's heart. God says so.

And now we need to hear the Shepherd's heartbeat, strong and steady, as he tightens his hold on us and carries us.

Heart Work

List your latest uncertainties about mothering. Name them as they rise within and just wait. Let your own needs surface, no different from those of a ewe with a new lamb. You need food, rest, water, and more rest. And you need a Shepherd to lead and sustain you. Wait with the Shepherd. You, too, are his lamb.

Heart Check

What do you need from the Good Shepherd?

At what specific times do you find it easy to believe God has your good at heart, that God carries you and your child close? When is that harder to do? In what instances have you experienced these two extremes?

In what ways do you tend to outrun the Shepherd's leading? What can you do to make yourself wait for that leading and provision?

Heart Cry

Dear Good Shepherd,
Am I really your lamb?
Really someone you lead, carry, feed, and rest?
Then why do I feel so alone,
So lonely,
So empty,
So weary?
Mothering leaves me baffled
And bewildered,
Lost in a wilderness
Uncharted by me
Or by my children.
Hold me tight.
Let me feel your heart pounding,
Wanting only my good
And the good of my children.
Would you let them hear your heartbeat, God?
Would you comfort them with your warm presence,
Though they may be far away from you?
Would you help them hear your heart,
Lord Jesus, Good Shepherd?
Would you tighten your arms around them,
Though they struggle to get away?
Lead on, kind Shepherd;
I will gladly rest
In your care.

Heart of God

Dear one,
I can hear your heartbeat
And the strange rhythm of trust and fear,
Of hope and doubt,
And the complicated beat
Of your fatigue.
Come to me.
Make a deliberate time today,
Right now,
To turn to me,
To trust me with your exhaustion
And all those strange rhythms
That comprise the song of motherhood.
I am the Good Shepherd,
And I will lead
And feed
And bring you rest.
And your lambs, too.
Just come to me.

Notes

1. Gina Stepp, "Give Sorrow More Than Words," Life & Health, *Vision*, winter 2007, http://www.vision.org/visionmedia/grief-and-loss/neuroscience/2166.aspx.

2. Dorothy A. Thrupp, "Savior, Like a Shepherd Lead Us," 1836, public domain.

Dear child, if you become wise, I'll be one happy parent.
My heart will dance and sing to the tuneful truth you'll speak.

—Proverbs 23:15–16 MSG

12

Heart Smart

When a lovely mom e-mailed me, I immediately related to her primary challenges: three girls, one in high school and two in college. That and stress. My first thought was, "Aw, she needs dark chocolate for her heart."

Well, research does say dark chocolate is good for the heart because it keeps all those free radicals from floating around inside the body and giving us all sorts of trouble, like heart disease. Chocolate comes from a plant, and a dark plant at that, which means chocolate is almost a vegetable. Too bad our moms didn't know that. Chocolate contains antioxidants that protect us from the aging impact of those radicals.

Good thing, those antioxidants, because this mothering business is not just hard on the heart. It gives us saggy bodies and wrinkles and gray hair long before grandchildren arrive to bless—and steal—our hearts. And even though the free radicals come about as a natural result of the digestive process, they have an electron that isn't stable.

Bouncing around within the body, it threatens us with heart problems and other chronic illnesses.[1]

We moms don't think about what's good for our hearts all that often. We worry about our kids' hearts no matter what their ages, and, if we have a spouse, his heart too. But our own hearts? Not only do women fail to recognize the symptoms of a heart attack, we also don't recognize when our own hearts show signs of attack from spiritual free radicals, those unstable emotional electrons that want to wreak havoc on our souls.

Above all else, guard your heart,
for everything you do flows from it.
—Proverbs 4:23

My new friend with the three teenage daughters is a good example. Thinking of her heart, she realized, "Whoa! I need some healing." Dark chocolate helped, I'm sure, but part of her smart-for-the-heart regime was counseling for a painful past. She'd also had some serious health issues, so pursuing better health for her heart and soul meant seeing a medical doctor then a specialist. Surgery followed.

Now en route to healing, she knows that the most helpful and godly and wise path through hard times is not to ignore her heart so she can get everyone else through the hard places. It's to pay attention to the condition of her own heart.

What wise choices can we make for our emotional and spiritual hearts, something that will work like dark chocolate for our souls? What feeds your spirit? What's the dark brown cocoa bean for your mother heart?

*And the peace of God, which transcends
all understanding, will guard your hearts
and your minds in Christ Jesus.*

—PHILIPPIANS 4:7

I look outside right now, the sun shining and reflecting off every surface. But on the other side of that glass, it's zero degrees with the wind chill, and the snow sparkles in drifts four or five feet high. Inside, the sun bounces off all that brightness, and I feel like a cat, ready to curl into a circle on the rug. The contentment of being in a warm, bright place is good for my heart, a good resting place for my soul.

Heart Work

Breathe deeply and invite God to fill your heart. Wait there, on a chest-expanding inhale, and ask God about your heart. Where is there neglect? Where does your heart need attention? Just wait and let the Holy Spirit point out your needs.

Heart Check

Where do you feel decidedly deficient in the wisdom department? What emotional free radicals associated with mothering have impacted your heart?

In what ways have you tried to be spiritually heart smart? Who supports you in that endeavor? Maybe an antioxidant session is in order with some of your friends. What could you do together that would be good for your heart?

What does your heart need? What do you gain by ignoring those needs? What feeds your heart? How and when are you feeding your

heart with poor supplies? What would nourish you, right now?
Today? This week?

Heart Cry

Dear God,
The free radicals of mothering
Are out to get me,
Get my heart,
Get my soul,
Get the best of me.
But I'm bringing my heart to you
And asking to be heart smart.
Help me to see my
Heart as you see it
And fill me with yourself,
Because then I will be
On the path toward wisdom.

Heart of God

Dear one,
Those free radicals of mothering
Got nothin' on me.
And I'm loving the flavonoids
That flood your system
When you feed your soul
Good food.
Breathe in the aroma,
Feast today
On the honey of my Word,
On the sweetness of being loved.
We'll tame those unruly radicals
One by one together.
Community is a powerful antioxidant.

Note

1. "Understanding Free Radicals and Antioxidants," Health Check Systems, accessed November 29, 2015, http://www.healthcheck systems.com/antioxid.htm.

Healing

Part 3

For a week I read and reread Matthew 8–9, which contains story after story of Jesus healing others. The stories reverberated in my heart like guitar strings plucked by heaven. A man with leprosy—healed. A Roman guard's servant—healed. Can you imagine it? Foreign troops occupy Judea and Jesus heals one of their servants! Peter's mother-in-law—healed. And "many who were demon-possessed were brought to [Jesus], and he drove out the spirits with a word and healed all the sick" (Matt. 8:16).

Many. The word sticks in my soul. The many who were brought to Jesus were healed.

The litany of healing continues in Matthew 9: the paralytic, a woman with a record-breaking menstrual bleed who'd lost all hope and all community, a dead girl—all healed. The eyes of the blind opened wide to see the Son of God. The tongue of the mute sprung loose to sing God's praises.

Jesus traveled throughout the region "teaching in their synagogues, proclaiming the good news of the kingdom and healing every disease and sickness" (Matt. 9:35). He preached about God's kingdom, and he demonstrated it by healing. Of course droves of people surrounded him, desperate to know that their current circumstances weren't all they could possibly expect. It was like a rowdy crowd jamming the service desk, demanding that someone make good on their money-back guarantee. And "when [Jesus] saw the crowds, he had compassion on them, because they were harassed and helpless, like sheep without a shepherd" (Matt. 9:36). *Compassion* means to suffer with. Jesus suffered with the people, his eyes opened to their emotional and physical pain.

He was despised and rejected by mankind,
a man of suffering, and familiar with pain. . . .
Surely he took up our pain and bore our suffering.

—Isaiah 53:3–4

Jesus understands desperation. He understands brokenness, despair, and grief. Jesus understands our broken hearts and our fractured or fracturing relationships, our hard pasts and our fears of the future. He sees; he knows. Jesus, who is the same yesterday, today, and forever, still views us with compassion.

Jesus healed then. Surely he heals now. The work of healing didn't end with the resurrection or the close of the New Testament, because Jesus doesn't change. God formed our bodies, fearfully and wonderfully, and designed us for healing. Our bodies are healing machines, given proper rest and nutrition. Despite our exposure to the toxins in the world, our bodies still heal. Even with the steady increase in environmental damage to our earth and to our food sources, our frames are still functional and self-healing. It's a miracle.

So it is with our hearts. God designed the heart for healing, for wholeness that is completed in heaven, where we will receive new bodies and no expiration date. Healing is a lifelong earthly journey because we're born with broken hearts, and our abandonment issues begin with the crushing exit from our mother's warm womb.

So the question is not "Can we be healed?" Emotional and spiritual healing is always possible. The prophets predicted the coming of the Messiah, who would rise with healing in his wings (see Mal. 4:2). Of course we can be healed. The real question is "Will we opt for personal healing when the needs around us call louder than our own; when those needing us are smaller and more helpless or older and increasingly helpless because of aging, will we choose to seek our own healing?" Personal healing may appear to be selfish rather than self-caring because it diverts our focus from people.

What would happen if we chose to model personal healing to the people around us who need hope? What choice do we have, if we want to become our best selves and to raise our children to be people of integrity?

It's easy to follow up on the question with a head nod and a thumbs up. Yes, by all means, let's heal so our kids have at least a shot at becoming healthy. But doing the work of healing is hard when facing grief, loss, the unexpected, stress, or disappointment in others, ourselves, and even God. I'd love to farm out this responsibility for my own healing. But it seems to be mine and mine alone. Except for one thing: God promised to help.

*Into the hovels of the poor, into the dark streets where the
homeless groan, God speaks: "I've had enough; I'm on
my way to heal the ache in the heart of the wretched."*

—PSALM 12:5 MSG

Returning to our walk through the gospel of Matthew, Jesus' next words clutch at my heart. After his heart flooded with compassion, he said, "The harvest is plentiful but the workers are few. Ask the Lord of the harvest, therefore, to send out workers into his harvest field" (Matt. 9:37–38). Where are the workers? Where are those who will bring hope to all these hurting people?

Jesus gives the answer immediately. Jesus' very next action was to call for the Twelve, sending them out as the team on which the entire gospel would be built and would travel throughout the world, eventually leading to you and me this very day (see Matt. 10:1). It was a team composed of mismatched people, some with very little education, some with huge tempers. They were a lot like us. But Jesus called them to be part of this huge healing movement that would change earth en route to heaven.

The Message renders Matthew 10:1, "He gave them power to kick out the evil spirits and to tenderly care for the bruised and hurt lives." To tenderly care—isn't that part of a mother's job? Yet sometimes we are the bruised and hurt lives. As we learn to tenderly care for our own wounds and bring them to the Great Physician, we can better care for the bruised and hurting people with whom we intersect.

As a result of speaking on military bases, I have learned that troops return from active duty in order to heal. And then deploy.

That seems like a good mission statement for mothers: heal and deploy.

"Even now," declares the LORD, "return to me with all your heart, with fasting and weeping and mourning." Rend your heart and not your garments. Return to the LORD your God, for he is gracious and compassionate, slow to anger and abounding in love.

—Joel 2:12–13

13
Rend Your Heart

A beautiful toddler from India, the tip of his head barely past his daddy's knee, bounced down the airport corridor. His thin arm stretched almost straight overhead to clutch his papa's hand. I watched with a slight grin, then a larger one, as they shared a bag of fresh, hot, chocolate chip cookies. With his clean new haircut, the boy's huge brown eyes appeared even larger than the cookies, like the size of the rising sun, or the moon when it hovers above the horizon. The boy's straight-edged bangs were perfect for a trip, perhaps to visit Grandma and Granddaddy, I thought.

The daddy-son duo joined a woman already in the waiting area. She welcomed them back with a smile that didn't quite convince me of her joy. Then tears filled her eyes and overflowed. She turned toward the window, as though to protect her son from her heart pain and to avoid spoiling his adventure. But turning away failed to stanch the waterfall.

From my anonymous perch a row behind them in the terminal, I cried with her, though she didn't know it. I wanted to bawl, to wrap my arms around her, and to ask, "Who died? I'm so sorry." Of course I didn't, and she finally dammed the tears and turned back to her family.

My sorrow is beyond healing, my heart is faint within me!
—JEREMIAH 8:18 NASB

Her husband glanced at his watch, then at his wife. He nodded, and the two rose and embraced with the child cradled between them, her tears falling again as they stood together in a trinity of sorts.

Then he left. He walked down the corridor and back out the exit and away from their lives. Reason unknown. The little boy screamed his heartbreak, his longing, and the mother's tears backed up somewhere in her soul so she could help her son with his grief. When he howled, she cupped her hand on his head and pressed her smooth cheek against his. When he started to reach out to strike her in his despair and helplessness, she grabbed his hand in a soft hold and whispered to him.

And I admired her. What a beautiful response. But I wondered, "When will it be time for her tears?"

[There is] a time to weep and a time to laugh,
a time to mourn and a time to dance.
—ECCLESIASTES 3:4

Sometimes when our hearts break, our first patch job is the split in our child's heart. We triage the ones with the most critical needs, and that is almost always our children. No matter our age as mothers or the ages of our children, their hearts get first response.

But when the soul emergency room settles down and the most vulnerable have received aid, it's time for our own soul triage. If we don't pay attention, the dam in our hearts holds back a reservoir of tears that finally bursts forth from the pressure. The tears, the loss, the pain will one day catch us unaware. Doctors often say, "If you don't cry, your body will." Maybe tears will surprise you in their form—migraines, back pain, stomach problems, or walls in relationships. Maybe as a coldness of soul born from the fear of loss. Maybe it takes the form of a dark depression or heart-pumping anger at God, at others, or at ourselves. It is so much better to cry out the pain early on and whenever the tears show up. My mother advised, "Sleep when the baby sleeps." Maybe we could modify that wisdom to "Cry when the baby cries" or "Cry when the baby sleeps."

Just so we make time for our tears.

Heart Work

Think back to some of those mother-child places of grief, pain, helplessness, or loss you have experienced, those airport departures where your tears could seep out for only a brief moment before you turned your attention to assuaging the pain of others. Wait with your own pain. Where did it come from? What was happening? If grief starts to erupt from that long-ignored heart place, wait with the tears. Don't try to blink or think them away. Just wait. There is a time for tears (see Eccl. 3:4). For your tears. And it just might be now.

Heart Check

How do you measure the level of tears in your heart? How often do you release some pressure on the dam and let the water levels recede? What does that look like for you?

What events represent waterlines on your heart walls? When do you notice them?

Who is a heart friend who could put her arms around you and "weep with those who weep"? How can you let her know you need a grief-and-loss, weep-and-wail session?

Heart Cry

Oh, God!
So often I rend my garments
And those of everyone else around me
Instead of my heart.
And I'm afraid to rend my heart,
Because maybe it will never stop
Rending and spilling
And I will drown in my tears and pain
And flood those around me.
Show me how to let my heart
Rip loose the tears.
Give me safe places to weep,
And your arms about me
To hold me in those tears.
For you are a God of compassion,
Abounding in love.
So I wait, now,
And trust you with my tears.
And with my rending heart.

Heart of God

Dear one,
There are good times
And better times
To leak those tears.
Either way,
Now is a perfect time
To assess the water levels
And the grief lines
In your heart and soul.
I take a handle-with-care approach with you
For just such a time
And wait even now
To have compassion on you.
Come, child.
Bring your tears,
Your grief,
Your sadness.
You can count on me
To weep with those who weep.
Rend your heart,
And I will repair those splits
In due time.

But you, Sovereign LORD, help me for your name's sake;
out of the goodness of your love, deliver me. For I am
poor and needy, and my heart is wounded within me.

—Psalm 109:21–22

14
A Heavy Heart

She smiled and nodded and touched people with her soft, kind hands. Her gray hair shone, a platinum crown about her sweet face. During a break at our retreat, she smiled and nodded and shook my hand. Then she ducked her head and asked in a hush, "You offered to talk with us individually." She hesitated, then her words came out, tentative and taut with worry—or pain. "Can I speak with you for a moment?"

We pulled away to a bench along the side of the multipurpose room, and I tucked her hand in mine. "Tell me, Marie."

Tears sputtered down her face, and she angled herself away from the crowd for privacy. "I have two children, and we all got along fine. We had a wonderful family. But after my husband died, my son stopped speaking to me. He won't visit me. He won't return my calls." After a deep and wobbling breath, she said, "I've asked him what's wrong. He just says, 'I'm busy with work.' But I'm his mother. What can I do?"

Her heaviness of heart showed on her face, in the faded blue of her eyes and the wrinkle between her brows. What would I do in her position? My heart would break too. I thought of all those years of mothering, all those scabbed knees and bike wrecks and girlfriend troubles, the broken window from the baseball, the hole in the wall from a little teenaged temper tantrum, and the move into a college dorm. How sad to think that all of that giving and loving and sacrificing and hoping, all the generosity of years dwindled off to nothing, to no relationship. We don't expect this as mothers. We would never believe the trail of years could lead to such fragmenting of the bond with our children.

*Restore us, LORD God Almighty; make your
face shine on us, that we may be saved.*
—PSALM 80:19

All weekend I'd been offering ways to deal with hard places in women's lives. I knew Marie had a pocket full of relevant notes and practical applications she could take action on when she got home. But I wanted to offer something personal, just for her.

"Could you stop by to see him?" I asked. I'm not a trained counselor, and I know it's not my job to fix people's pain. But stop by? That seemed simple enough, and it's what I would do as a mom in that situation. I'd drive to his house and knock on his door like the persistent widow in Luke 18. At least, I think I would.

She shook her head. "He's three hours away. And he told me, 'Don't come see me, Mom.'" The tears spurted again, and she tried to control her sobs. "And . . . he hasn't talked to his sister in ten years. They used to be close. I don't know." Her throat closed around the words, and she wept in silent loneliness and sorrow.

I put a stopper in the questions that poured into my mother mind, questions like "Is he involved in a questionable or immoral lifestyle? Does he have a girlfriend living with him you don't know about? Could he be lying about his job or his success? Is he ashamed of himself? Did he abuse his sister?" Speculating about the lives of others is an endless and unhelpful occupation, and it's a distraction from the real point: to understand our own heart and needs. "You can't do this alone," I said. "Do you have a friend to help you in your pain?" I knew she was regarded as the backbone of her little farm community in the rural Midwest.

"No one knows," she whispered, her fingers forming a grate over her mouth. "I can't tell them. I'm so ashamed and embarrassed."

Restore us to yourself, LORD, that we may return;
renew our days as of old.

—LAMENTATIONS 5:21

I wrapped my arms around her, worried about her health. "Oh, Marie. That must hurt so much. I'm so sad for you. And for him." Some things we just can't fix, and it makes our hearts heavy, like a tractor tire filled with cement. All we can do is crawl to God's knees and dump the pain there. I prayed for her then, asking God to comfort her sore mother heart, to bring her son to God's heart, and to heal them both. Her soft hand kept slipping away to backhand the tears from her cheeks.

Heart Work

What is your tractor tire, that unexpected, huge trial in your mothering life that you could not have anticipated? Oh, the weight on these fragile instruments, our hearts, the emotional heaviness. Name your tire issue and carefully roll it to Jesus. You cannot do anything about it. But Jesus can carry it for you. Now wait for the relief to appear.

Heart Check

Give words to the weight you carry. Try saying its name and describing it aloud. This makes the issue more real, releasing the internal pressure of pain it causes. Naming your trial frees space for hope as well.

Has your pain turned to shame, to a sense that you are a failure? When and how did that happen?

Who else knows this painful truth about you, about your journey, your parenting, your child? We need companions who will accompany us, friends who know the way because they've been down that road. Who can help hear your heart? When will you share your burden with her?

Heart Cry

Oh, God.
It hurts to put this into words,
This heaviness of heart,
This sense of failure
As a mother,
As a woman.
Hear my heart,
Even if no one else does.
Please.
Out of the goodness of your love,
Deliver me,
Deliver my beloved child.
Take this weight from me,

This tractor tire of pain
Lashed around my heart
And carry it.
Carry me.

Heart of God

Dear one,
One nice thing about tires
Is that they roll.
So roll it my way,
And maybe even
Hop aboard.
Burn some rubber,
And let's head toward healing
Together.
I know the way.
Just aim toward me.

"And now, here's what I'm going to do: I'm going to start all over again.
I'm taking her back out into the wilderness where we had our first date,
and I'll court her. I'll give her bouquets of roses. I'll turn Heartbreak Valley
into Acres of Hope. She'll respond like she did as a young girl, those
days when she was fresh out of Egypt," . . . this is GOD's Message.

—Hosea 2:14–16 MSG

15
Mending the Broken Heart

She waved him off; he snapped a sharp salute as the flag waved
its own salute in the brisk wind. She waved, the flag waved, and every
snap struck her heart like a sniper's bullet. Like so many mothers
before her, she waved off her son under the flag of her country as he
deployed, so brave and handsome and fit, to bring the world to peace.

When he died in Iraq, her heart splintered and then went numb,
deadened by the loss, the sorrow, the heartsickness of a life gone
too soon, a life barely lived. A hole in the world was created by the
loss of this young man, so fresh from his mother's heart.

Broken heart syndrome [takotsubo cardiomyopathy] is
a temporary heart condition that's often brought on
by stressful situations, such as the death of a loved one.
People with broken heart syndrome may have sudden
chest pain or think they're having a heart attack.[1]

Like generations of mothers throughout the ages whose children have been too soon removed from them—whether by accident, enemy fire, addiction, disease, or something else—this mother hadn't counted on the loss of her son. Mothers should not outlive their children. This club has no willing members. Neither does the club for mothers with other kinds of lost children—those who lost their way, lost their faith, lost contact with family, lost their foothold on reality, or lost their own hearts; kids who've lost hope and are barely hanging on; kids who lost hope and then took their own lives.

Healing from heartbreak seems impossible, maybe even undesirable. Does healing mean forgetting the one we loved—love—so much, who took up so much room in our hearts, thoughts, and daily lives? Does it mean finding a way to relinquish that life or to say, "I'm over it now"? That's something that absolutely never happens, according to the mothers I've known whose children died.

The timeline of heartbreak looks like it belongs to Methuselah, and its trajectory resembles the stock market crash of 1929. For my friend whose son died in the war, months passed before she could challenge God with those fist-shaking, where-were-you questions. And many months more before she could return to the possibility of faith. She still cries, nearly two years later, and is learning that no one knows how to handle a brokenhearted, broken mother. Heartbreak has plowed deep furrows in her marriage and family.

But [Jesus] said to me, "My grace is sufficient for you,
for my power is made perfect in weakness."
Therefore I will boast all the more gladly about my
weaknesses, so that Christ's power may rest on me.

—2 Corinthians 12:9

She too often feels lost—to God, to her friends and family, and sometimes to herself. But when her pastor challenged her to look for signs of God's love every day, she polished her binoculars. She struggles to feel and to heal, but once in a while she glimpses God's love in her peripheral vision. She finds it in an e-mail from a friend or an encounter along the way.

The questions still lead nowhere except to silence, and the hurt sometimes keeps her awake at night. But as she sees God's love flash by like the wing of a bluebird in flight, she knows she is not lost. God has never lost sight of her, even though she cannot see him.

She feels that pulse, the heartbeat of God, as she watches. And sometimes she thinks she will make it on this journey toward healing. She holds Jesus' mission statement and promise from Isaiah 61:1 in her clenched fist: "The Spirit of the Sovereign LORD is on me, because the LORD has anointed me to proclaim good news to the poor. He has sent me to bind up the brokenhearted, to proclaim freedom for the captives and release from darkness for the prisoners." That's a heart promise worth claiming.

Heart Work

As you settle down, let your heart's cry rise to the surface. Look for those places of intense pain, of howling loss, of subtle aching. And if tears come, let them. Pray for their coming because weeping primes the pump of healing. And as you weep, weep not as one who has no hope. Instead, envision the invisible God surrounding you, holding you as a parent holds a brokenhearted child. For God encloses us behind and before, and he comes alongside us. The Holy Spirit wraps around us with a holy presence. So rest there, your heartache rising to the surface, and maybe your tears too.

Heart Check

Who is or has been—or feels—lost to you, lost to your heart or your life? If this is not your personal experience, perhaps it is one of your deepest fears, that someone you love, like a child, will be lost to you. When you feel that sense of loss, what do you do with it?

Perhaps you are the lost child. To whom are you lost? Yourself? Your parents? Others? In what ways do you feel lost to God? Do you ever feel as though you've lost God or lost your faith? Which of your life experiences have challenged your belief in a God who loves and cares and answers prayers?

Where do you glimpse God's love throughout the day? Keep track of those sightings. This is one of the ways God heals the heartbroken, by showing flashes of love.

Heart Cry

I'm a little tired of Heartbreak Valley, God.
Sometimes this heartbreak
Is more than I can take,
The darkness too dark
And the silence too resonant
And my heart too battered.
So many unanswered prayers,
So many disappointments,
So much fear,
I can barely look you in the face
Let alone trust you again.
But I cling to this with the little faith I have left:
Though you feel lost to me,
You have never lost sight of me.
Find me, God,
Because I cannot find myself,
And my heart is MIA.
Though there may be no answers

This side of heaven,
Let me see the flashes of your love
Until this heartbreak heals.
Mend this broken heart,
The needle of your love
Stitching in and out of the folds of my life,
Pulling the pieces of my heart
Back together.

Heart of God

Dear one,
Even in this desert of loss,
Watch for those bouquets
And the flash of bird wings.
Expect the unexpected,
A telegram of my love, my care,
By plane, by bird, by special delivery.
Keep watch.
I'm on duty,
And I promise
Healing is the order of the day.
It's what I do.
That, and love you.

Note

1. "Broken Heart Syndrome," Mayo Clinic, March 1, 2014, http://www.mayoclinic.org/diseases-conditions/broken-heart-syndrome/basics/definition/con-20034635.

Jesus replied . . . "But the Advocate, the Holy Spirit, whom the Father will send in my name, will teach you all things and will remind you of everything I have said to you. Peace I leave with you; my peace I give you. I do not give to you as the world gives. Do not let your hearts be troubled and do not be afraid."

—John 14:23, 26–27

16
A Troubled Heart

Numerous wives from a nearby military base attended the parenting group where I was privileged to meet such brave mothers. The table conversation turned to the difficulty of parenting in military families. Angie said, "My husband is on permanent disability after serving in Afghanistan." Post-traumatic stress disorder (PTSD) rendered him incapable of holding a job. But when he erupted in uncontrollable rage, specialists diagnosed him with a traumatic brain injury (TBI) from being so close to explosives for an extended period.[1]

Their young marriage exploded, and Angie's troubled heart needed a safe distance from her husband. She had to leave temporarily with their five-year-old son so they could all begin to heal. Then, one day God got Angie's attention and directed her heart to Jesus' words: "Do not let your hearts be troubled. You believe in God; believe also in me" (John 14:1).

The problem with trouble is that it's so personal. The troubles on the other side of the world don't impact us too much emotionally and spiritually until someone we love is there trying to stop the troubles.

*Hearts will never be practical until they
can be made unbreakable.*

—L. FRANK BAUM[2]

Our hearts get troubled easily in this troubling world, even though Jesus said, "In this world you will have trouble. But take heart! I have overcome the world" (John 16:33). That's great to know, but what do we do with our hearts in the meantime, when our own world seems to be spinning out of control with explosive (or implosive) people or situations, when the difficult issues are enough to make us want to run away from home? When Jesus made this statement, it was less of an announcement and more of an order. In the midst of his troubled disciples who were mulling all the prophecies he had just given them, Jesus' next words were essentially, "Don't be troubled. Don't let yourself."

Is being troubled really a choice? Because experiencing trouble sure doesn't seem to be a choice, not for any responsible parent I know. But Jesus doesn't just tell us what not to do. He doesn't just say, "Don't be troubled." That would be like saying, "Don't worry; be happy. Everything is going to be all right." Nope, Jesus knows us better than that. He knows that if we don't have something to replace the troubling feeling in our souls, then our hearts might blow or fibrillate until we collapse.

*Never be afraid to trust an unknown
future to a known God.*

—CORRIE TEN BOOM[3]

The alternative is changing the focus, pulling it from the trouble, from our insufficiency and lack of wisdom and parental bankruptcy, from the emotions and fear. Jesus points us in another direction: "You've trusted in God. Now, trust in me" (see John 14:1). Turn from trouble to trust, to Jesus. Look at his life: He came to this world as a baby, had human parents, and suffered a great deal of trouble. But, except in the garden of Gethsemane, Christ never appeared to have been troubled by his own state or fate. Why? Maybe because of his intimate knowledge of and trust in God. In spite of all the trouble that came to Jesus on the heels of giving this commandment to us—because he surely knew trouble was up next on his agenda—he showed he had what we need: absolute trust in God.

Angie, whose husband suffered violent outbursts, took Jesus at his word, and the family is back together. Facing both the normal troubles of parenting and the deeply troubling effects of PTSD and TBI, Angie turned her focus from the difficulties and pain to create a plan of active trust. She met with counselors personally, and then she and her husband received couples' therapy. Together they chose a healing path that includes good boundaries and trigger alerts. They also sought companions on the journey, military couples who'd bumped down that troubled road themselves. Friends at the parenting group bolster her and provide hope in the midst of trouble. Though it's a bit like jogging in a field of land mines, she keeps coming back to Jesus, who said, "Do not let your hearts be troubled." She has trusted in God. She will trust also in Jesus.

Heart Work

Sometimes troubles sink to the bottom of our hearts and need some stirring to rise up into our notice again. In the quiet, ask the Advocate to remind you where trouble skulks along the bottom of your soul. You're not stirring up trouble just to make the muck thicker; you're inviting God to help you notice the trouble and then replace that trouble with courage, trust, and peace. Take it slow, though. Hurry only makes more mud.

Heart Check

Sometimes we or others interpret Jesus' words to mean "Buck up, look on the bright side, get over it." In what circumstances has Jesus' command not to be troubled seemed like a platitude to you? How have you or others used those words insincerely?

Practically speaking, how do you make the pivot in your heart from trouble to trust? What is hard about that? In what ways have you trusted God? Have you found yourself feeling safe or let down?

In what troubles do you need to make a decisive change of focus? How will you create a plan for active trust? Who accompanies you on the pitted road to "Don't worry; trust in me"?

Heart Cry

Dear God!
This is more than I bargained for
When I said "I do" to being a mother.
I didn't know that also meant
Yes, I do
To the traumas of relationship,
To the disappointments of humanity
And troubled hearts,

My own and those of the people I love.
But today,
Right now,
I take you literally,
Believe you when you say
You have overcome the world.
And my own world is not too big for you
Nor my troubles too little for you to bother.
So please take my troubled heart
In your hand
And redirect my gaze from my pain
To your peace and provision.
Because I cannot do this
Without you.
Today,
Right now
For this moment,
I choose to trust you.

Heart of God

Dear one,
I know the troubles you've seen.
From troubled to trusting takes time
And practice,
But it becomes a habit.
Where have you found me faithful?
Where have you seen my care?
Remember the next time you feel troubled.
That's your trigger
To turn to me.
From troubled to trusting takes time,
But we have all the time
In the world.
And now
Is the best of times
To trust.

Notes

1. For more information on PTSD and TBI in a military setting, see woundedwarriorproject.org.

2. "The Wonderful Wizard of Oz Quotes," Goodreads.com, accessed February 25, 2016, https://www.goodreads.com/work/quotes/1993810-the-wonderful-wizard-of-oz.

3. Corrie ten Boom, "Quotes about Trust," Goodreads.com, accessed November 29, 2015, http://www.goodreads.com/quotes/tag/trust.

Let the word of Christ richly dwell within you, with all wisdom
teaching and admonishing one another with psalms and hymns and
spiritual songs, singing with thankfulness in your hearts to God.

—Colossians 3:16 NASB

17

An Aching Heart

At my annual exam (yes, that one), Millie the Wonder Nurse
asked her usual questions about my health. She checked my blood
pressure and my temperature, then eyeballed me. "And are you under
any stress lately?"

My heart fluttered. Tears spurted into my eyes, and I opened them
wide to keep them from overflowing. "Why do you ask?" Had she
seen some sort of panic correlation between her intake questions and
my body's responses?

When you are physically active, excited, or ill,
your heart rate can rise significantly.
This is a natural response.[1]

Millie smiled. "Just part of holistic health." She looked at me again.
"Are you?"

I sucked extra air into what felt like collapsing lungs. I stammered and cleared my throat. "Well, I had a little auto accident earlier this year. Still in PT for that. Our son's in a really hard place." My voice shrank to a whisper; it was all the air I could force out. "He told us we never really loved him. Uh, also, a heavy travel season for work." In my mind, I added, "And our daughter's getting married, out of state. And we have three bridal showers in three states, and I'm hosting two of them, and . . . and . . ."

We all have stressors, your list is probably worse and longer than mine, and our hearts interpret even happy events in our lives as stress—even positive stress registers as stress. Research suggests that stress impacts our hearts. This indispensable instrument reacts to stress by increasing its rate, speeding up the flow of blood, and bumping up our blood pressure. To create necessary fight-or-flight energy, stress triggers the dumping of fatty acids into our bloodstream, raising our triglyceride and cholesterol levels. When stress is chronic, the body continues to pump out cortisol, which may direct where fat is deposited in the body, usually in the abdomen.[2] Oh, happy day.

The heart does the most physical work of any muscle during a lifetime. The power output of the heart ranges from one to five watts. While the quadriceps can produce one hundred watts for a few minutes, an output of one watt for eighty years is equal to 2.5 gigajoules.[3]

So my aching heart is a whole health problem. I'm not crazy about this. I want to learn how to live well in this mothering profession, with its often-chronic stress that leads to aching heart syndrome. Of course stress is bigger than that which comes from parenting, and it attacks us from all sides, compounding its effect on our bodies. Our hearts depend on us to find a better way to live.

King David taught me in Psalm 10, 13, and 15 that when arrows fly at us from all directions, thanksgiving is a cure for the aching, stressed-out heart. Many psalms begin with David's woes, which he recounts, but then he redirects his heart to God's faithful provision. David looked around and saw all God had done, and his heart resumed normal beating. Maybe it is impossible to be stressed and thankful at the same time.

Today, I'm going to write down as many thanksgivings as possible in sixty seconds. Not that the stressors on my aching heart aren't real. They are, and I can't change them. But I can change how I—and eventually my heart—respond to the stress.

Heart Work

Sixty seconds isn't much time when considering your reasons to be thankful. Grab your journal or a piece of paper and a pen. List the stressors creating your heavy heart. Reread it and take a moment to feel the anxiety of that weight, to notice your heart. Then set a timer for one minute. Below the list you just made, write everything you can think of to be thankful for. Now wait with your heart and turn that thankful list into praise to God.

Heart Check

How do you normally handle stress? What toll does it take on your aching heart? Your family?

Regarding the Heart Work exercise above, what does it feel like to have your aching heart poured out on paper in the open? When you look at your list, what emotions arise? Guilt? Shame? More anxiety?

How can you shift from an aching heart to a thankful one without being a fake mother?

Heart Cry

Oh God,
Sometimes my heart aches within me.
I feel the pain of this impossible, glorious
Profession of mothering
In the center of my chest,
And it hurts.
So I lift my eyes to you,
And I look around at your
Kind provisions for me
And for my children,
And I wait,
Humbly,
For you to ease the pressure
On this frail heart.
Thank you
For your unfailing love.

Heart of God

Dear one,
Thank you
Is a good place to start
And a good place to land
To combat the inevitable
Stress we call life
In this troubled world.
Fight back against the soul dumping
With words of thank you,
Words of praise.
And if you can't think of any,
Open up to David's words,
Just about any page will do,
Because he learned to

Combat stress
With thank you,
And so can you.
Meanwhile,
I am thankful too.
For you.

Notes

1. "How Your Heart Works," Heart Foundation, accessed February 25, 2016, http://heartfoundation.org.au/your-heart/how-your-heart-works.
2. Christine A. Maglione-Garves, Len Kravitz, and Susanne Schneider, "Cortisol Connection: Tips on Managing Stress and Weight," The University of New Mexico, accessed November 29, 2015, https://www.unm.edu/~lkravitz/Article%20folder/stresscortisol.html.
3. "36 Interesting Facts About . . . The Human Heart," Random History.com, posted January 28, 2010, http://facts.randomhistory.com/human-heart-facts.html.

I sat there in despair, my spirit draining away, my heart heavy,
like lead. I remembered the old days, went over all you've done,
pondered the ways you've worked, stretched out my hands
to you, as thirsty for you as a desert thirsty for rain.

—Psalm 143:4–6 MSG

18

Heart-to-Heart

Sometimes parenting feels like waiting for the other shoe to drop. After a while, I wonder how many feet this shoe dropper has, or at least how many pairs of shoes. It's like the sky is raining pumps and boots and flip-flops and stilettos.

One summer seemed especially full of dropping footwear, a Jurassic Park for cobblers. I wanted to duck under awnings and porches but always seemed to be in the drop zone with no helmet. My children returned from various points around the country and were at last old enough and mature enough to share, heart-to-heart, about some painful times in their young lives, times that would have been made easier, though not prevented, if I'd known what was happening.

Hopefully, failure really is the mother of success.
If so, our kids should be in good shape.

As a mother, I'd been unaware of the perils the kids encountered, the damage it had done, and their ricochet reactions to it. I leapt to take the blame, immediately whispering in a choked voice, "I'm so sorry I failed you."

One child, so wise, asked in frustration, "Why do you always do that? You always turn attention on yourself. Couldn't you just say, 'How horrible that was for you. How frightened, hurt, confused, you must have been'?" That I didn't immediately offer such a compassionate response compounded my child's hurt.

We moms wouldn't hurt our children for the world, even on our most incompetent days, not on purpose. To know they endured pain without talking to us, without receiving our protective covering, to know that their silence or distance or rebellion or anger covered up such agony is heartbreaking. Is our heartbreak a selfish reaction too?

The next day, my family expected fifteen to twenty people for a birthday picnic. So after the kids' words, I went outside to work in the yard, the temperatures high and my agony for my children even higher. I mopped sweat from my brow and prayed for my kids, prayed over the new revelations of old pain from their pasts and the new shapes of that morphing pain. As I prayed, I desperately grieved for their agony, still sorrowful for my neglectful ignorance.

My flesh and my heart may fail, but God is the strength of my heart and my portion forever.
—Psalm 73:26

Then somehow, from somewhere, I felt or heard these words: "I have paid for the pain."

I stopped working and straightened. Then I rolled back onto the ground, threw my arms out on either side, and wept.

Subconsciously, I realized my body formed a cross there on the spiky green grass, the sky bright above me. As I waited, the anguish over failing my children faded, and I felt only their pain. Then I named aloud the hard times in their lives that I knew of. And I heard Jesus say, "I was there." Absolute relief filled me. They were not alone in those dreadful times.

The next morning, my devotional reading contained John Chrysostom's words: "Were he distant from us in place, you might well doubt, but if God is present everywhere, to him that strives and is in earnest he is near. . . . What father would ever be thus obedient to his offspring? What mother is there, so ready and continually standing, in case her children call her? There is not one, no father, no mother, but God stands continually waiting."[1]

Then this psalm, that bright morning, that birthday party day, chased the clouds of darkness away: "God makes everything come out right; he puts victims back on their feet. . . . God's love . . . is ever and always, eternally present to those who fear him, making everything right for them and their children" (Ps. 103:6, 17–18 MSG).

What a wonderful reason to throw a party. I rose, smiling, and set up the tables for the birthday picnic.

Heart Work

We are all victims of life in a broken world. You are no different from your child. As you settle into the quiet of Christ's presence, ask him to show you how he's worked, to show you all he has done on your behalf. Listen to your heavy heart and wait with that weight until the load begins to lighten because of his faithfulness and capability.

Heart Check

What are some of those heavy-heart places you wish you could have talked with your own mother about? Perhaps you did talk with her; how did she respond? How do you wish she'd responded? Can you talk to her about them now?

One mom's children saw her as perfect and felt unable to share their own struggles with her. How about your own mothering? What are some of the heart-to-hearts you've had with your children? Perhaps they aren't yet old enough to share their own perspectives on difficult times. How then can you invite them into more openness about their personal lives?

Take time to stretch out your hands to God. Roll onto your back on the floor if that helps. What are you offering up?

Heart Cry

Dear God,
I name aloud the hard times in my life
And in the lives of my family,
And my heart hurts.
I would take away the pain.
I would have been there.
I meant to be there.
I tried to be.
And into this echoing abyss
I hear your words:
"I have paid for their pain."
The anguish of my own guilt halts.
I name the pain—
My painful places,
My children's—
And your voice whispers again:
"I was there. I was there."
Your love pours over me,

A beam of relief.
They were not—
Are not—alone.
My heart immediately rises
Like active leaven
And lightens.
Today really is
A perfect day
For a party.

Heart of God

Dear one,
I've paid for their pain
And yours.
Your mistakes were inevitable;
Your inability to be present
In all the trials and heartaches,
Normal because you are human.
But I am not limited
By time and space,
And I was there.
I am there now,
With them,
With you,
And I promise
There is no condemnation
For you who have hidden yourself
In my love.
So come along.
It's time to celebrate
Your freedom.

Note

1. Thomas Oden and Cindy Crosby, eds., "Merciful and Just," in *Ancient Christian Devotional: A Year of Weekly Readings*, Lectionary Cycle C (Downers Grove, IL: InterVarsity Press 2009), 197.

Community

Part 4

High crime, high unemployment, and low income created a perfect storm of self—self-centeredness and family-centeredness—for my insular little self during the early years of ministry for my husband and me. On my daily walks to the local grade school, me bumping the too-short stroller with my too-long legs, I reflected on my life of cheering on my children toward integrity and joy in an economically difficult and decidedly pessimistic area. It was taking its toll on me. And on the kids. Oh, and on my marriage.

I became so preoccupied with my own family and our little personal issues that I didn't remember the mom who struggled to keep her family together in the tiny, tumbledown house on the hill. Her husband disappeared except when he needed her paycheck. She was an alcoholic, and he gambled. Her great hope was that one day they would win the lottery so she could insulate the house and keep her kids warm. That was on the days when she didn't want to kill her husband because he'd used the car's hubcaps to settle a gambling debt.

And that was just one house with one little family in our crowded urban neighborhood.

Mothering expanded my heart beyond myself but, ironically, isolated me within my family's needs and schedule. In that kind of isolation, we become so aware of our own shortcomings and so certain we don't know the right next thing for our children that parenting feels like a guessing game, a gamble, or even a good joke at times. At other times, the walk of faith feels like a tightrope made of old cotton thread, so thin and fragile it can't possibly support our weight.

During those years, I felt inadequate and alone. Misery loves to isolate.

The worst part of holding the memories is not the pain. It's the loneliness of it. Memories need to be shared.

—Lois Lowry[1]

One of the Enemy's most effective deceptions, because it feels so true, is that we are alone in our questions, pain, shame, and mistakes. No one else has these problems. No one else makes mistakes. We are all alone.

Through these years of parenting, even as my children graduated from the rocking chair and sippy cup to holding hands while crossing streets to curfews and caps and gowns, I have learned the rock-bottom concept that has been true since the genesis of time: It is not good to be alone. Since college days, I've had just a few party friends—the "Let's go shopping! Let's go to the spa!" friends—but numerous accountability friends. This group of wise women has both nurtured me and told me when I was off-roading spiritually and relationally. I've had prayer partners who knew more about me than anyone else in my life and writer friends who invited me into the joyous sorority of honing words to communicate truth, and who then became soul friends. I've had artist friends, a mother friend, and a spiritual challenger friend.

I have a dream too, but it's about singing and dancing and making people happy. It's the kind of dream that gets better the more people you share it with. And I found a whole group of friends who have the same dream, and that makes us sort of like a family.

—KERMIT THE FROG[2]

These courageous women formed an army about me, relieved my unfair and unrealistic pressures I put on my husband and children to meet all my emotional and spiritual needs, and, in love, invited me forward on the journey toward wholeness and holiness. Community invites us into transformation. It draws us out of the tight walls and exclusiveness of those intense mothering years.

Wounds from a friend can be trusted.
—PROVERBS 27:6

Parenting can limit our focus and hinder our common sense and reason. It can blind us to the bigger picture, the world beyond our flesh and blood. King David's numerous wives birthed numerous sons, and while David was a great leader, renowned in history, he was not consistently an exemplary parent. This gives me hope, given my own imperfections and inconsistencies as a parent. God still saw fit to allow David to be Jesus' great-great-great-great-great grandfather.

Some of David's sons displayed self-centered, even evil, tendencies. One son, Absalom, the son with famously gorgeous hair, started a coup, trying to wrest the kingdom from his father. A civil war ensued, with family fighting family and David's men fighting his son and his insurrectionists. There was nothing "civil" about it.

During a mad chase, Absalom's horse ran under a low-branched tree, and Absolom's gorgeous hair caught in the branches, unseating him from the horse. He dangled from the tree until one of David's soldiers found him. David's man ran Absalom through with his sword, believing his actions to be in the king's, and the kingdom's, best interest.

When messengers brought that news to David, bragging about the conquest, David dissolved in grief for his son. His heartbroken words, "O my son Absalom! O Absalom, my son, my son!" (2 Sam. 19:4), have become the enduring symbol of a father's grief for his wayward son. The troops tiptoed about in shame, completely disheartened, as if they'd been the defectors rather than the loyal victors. Despite their quashing the coup, securing the kingdom, and saving the rest of David's family, the king lost himself in grief over the death of his traitorous son. He also very nearly lost his army.

But David's accountability man, Joab, rebuked him. His words in 2 Samuel 19:5–7 exemplify the truth-telling we all need occasionally from someone who knows us, someone with a broad perspective on our lives, relationships, and responsibilities, someone not afraid to risk offending us in order to help us be the people we were created to be in the roles we've been given. Because of their long relationship and his position in David's life and leadership, Joab deserved the right to speak plainly.

David's grief was real and valid. He needed to grieve. Joab's words do not deny that reality. But Joab spoke for his king's larger roles and the big picture. He spoke the truth with force but also with respect. David could have made the worst mistake of his entire life; if he didn't rectify it, not a man would be left standing with him by nightfall.

"Get hold of yourself; get out there and put some heart into your servants!" Joab told him (2 Sam. 19:7 MSG).

As we surround ourselves with people who love us and call us forward, people who refresh our hearts, we are strengthened and challenged to do the same—to get out there and put some heart into the people filling the world around us.

That's real transformation. We are changed for the good of others.

Notes

1. Lois Lowry, *The Giver* (New York: Houghton Mifflin Harcourt, 1993), 193.
2. "Movie Quotes About Friendship," Beliefnet.com, accessed February 26, 2016, http://www.beliefnet.com/Entertainment/Movies/2010/02/Friendship-Movie-Quotes. aspx?b=1&p=10.

This is how we know we're living steadily and deeply in him, and he in us: He's given us life from his life, from his very own Spirit. Also, we've seen for ourselves and continue to state openly that the Father sent his Son as Savior of the world. Everyone who confesses that Jesus is God's Son participates continuously in an intimate relationship with God. We know it so well, we've embraced it heart and soul, this love that comes from God.

—1 John 4:13–16 MSG

19
Heart and Soul

Her arms were as thin as paperclips as she wrapped them around her chest. She scarcely looked old enough to graduate high school, let alone attend a group for mothers of young children. I'd planted myself like a lamppost after the meeting to talk with women, hoping for a soul connection with them after speaking on heart care for moms.

When my children graduated from diapers and I realized there were no easy answers or guaranteed systems for raising kids, I stopped speaking about parenting techniques. But heart and soul—that's more than a tune by Hoagy Carmichael. That's life or death. If we don't take care of our hearts, how will we stay alive, let alone raise our children? Babies will steal our hearts and souls—and let's not talk about the teenagers. Unless we refill them regularly, we end up exhausted, lonely, empty.

The audience had been stiff, the atmosphere stifled, and I wondered how much was related to the economics of that county, one of the wealthiest in the nation. Whatever was going on, they didn't laugh, they didn't cry, and they sure weren't buying the books designed for real women who need to do both.

Keep in mind that to avoid loneliness, many people need both a social circle and an intimate attachment. Having just one of the two may still leave you feeling lonely.

—GRETCHEN RUBIN[1]

So I stood, hoping, smiling, silently praying as the women mingled with one another. At least, I thought they opted for community, because we are, after all, stronger together than separate. And they chose community for their own sake, another plus in their favor. Then along came this thin-as-a-minute young mom. She swayed in baby-rock motion, from foot to foot, though her arms were empty. I couldn't imagine her tiny frame pregnant, yet she said, "I have a fifteen-month-old in the nursery. She was a whoops."

Waving graceful hands, she seemed flustered. Words tumbled out. "I grew up in church, then left and became sexually active. Then I got pregnant. My boyfriend and I are together, most of the time. Except when he abuses me, and then I leave for a week or two."

All it takes, sometimes, is a kind look and tenderness. Her tears must have been waiting for just such a moment because they popped from her eyes and slid down her cheeks. She pressed the tears away, but they refused to stop.

"It's not working. I'm exhausted and lonely. I love my baby, but I'm so scared." She turned from me, selected four books, then clutched them to her slender frame. "I've started coming to church again. God is what I need. Just last night I told God, 'I need something just for me.'" She gulped, swallowing hard. "I'm so tired of feeling alone."

What should young people do with their lives today?
Many things, obviously. But the most daring thing
is to create stable communities in which the
terrible disease of loneliness can be cured.

—KURT VONNEGUT[2]

"And unloved?" I asked.

She nodded, tightening her hold on the books. "It's time to take care of my own soul." She tried again to smooth away her tears, but the reservoir had been filling for far too long. "I'm sorry for crying."

"Tears are good. Sometimes tears are the beginning of heart and soul care. If you can cry, your heart will stay alive." I patted and hugged her, whispering a prayer.

When she ran to pick up her daughter, she held the books to her chest like a life ring. "I think I'm coming home."

In that dim fellowship hall, with its emphasis on community, her smile had hope for the first time all day.

Heart Work

Silence is one of the ways to tend heart and soul. As you settle in, listening to your heart, ask the Holy Spirit to show you the lonely, scared, hurt, empty, exhausted places. Next, just be still. Invite God to comfort, soothe, fill, and restore you. And then just wait.

Heart Check

When is heart and soul care difficult for you? In what ways does the lack of care affect you? What stops you from seeking this kind of nurture?

How does it impact your loved ones when you haven't had time or created time for your heart and soul?

What does it look like to tend to your heart and soul? How will you fit it into your life? At what times do you just need someone to hug you and hold you in your tears? Who does that for you?

Heart Cry

Dear God!
I press them back
But still they pour out,
These tears
That speak of my emptiness,
My loneliness,
My despair.
How do I go forward,
Heart and soul,
When the needs around me
Are bigger than I am?
I wait there
With that thought—
My heart and soul needs
Are bigger than I am—
But you are bigger still.
And so I have come
To the right place
At just the right time.
Help me to honor
My heart and soul
By taking time with you.
Meet me here
In this empty place,
For you are
Bigger than my fears,
Bigger than my tears,
And able to hold
My heart and soul
Together.

Heart of God

Dear one,
Tend to heart and soul,
And you'll find that I provide
All you need,
Just for you,
To grow and live and love.
And to laugh again.
Sometimes it takes tears.
It always requires community;
In fact you are always
In community
With me.
Today
I hope you will notice
And pay close attention
To the mending
Of heart and soul.

Notes

1. Lorenzo Jenson III, "36 Absolutely Heartbreaking Quotes About Loneliness," Thought Catalog, March 16, 2015, http://thoughtcatalog.com/lorenzo-jensen-iii/2015/03/36-absolutely-heartbreaking-quotes-about-loneliness/.
2. Ibid.

The LORD is close to the brokenhearted and
saves those who are crushed in spirit.

—Psalm 34:18

10
The Mosaic Heart Work

We stood in line at the airport in boarding lane 2. The woman behind me sighed and shrugged after a college exploration trip with her son. In that act universal to almost-adults, he had ducked his head and moved away, seeking invisibility, disconnecting himself from his mother to appear more sophisticated. He waited thirty people behind her in line. She rearranged her gaping, over-stuffed purse, pointing to a crisp white bakery bag. "I have cookies for him, anyway." She paused. "He'll get it one day," she said. "What I've done for him."

"Eventually. They have no idea what it costs to be a mother." I smiled at her, feeling apologetic for her pain, hoping my words were true. It's not easy having children who think they deserve the moon simply because they exist. It's not easy being a mother who wants her children to have the moon either.

A woman across the ropes in boarding lane 1 nodded. The circles under her eyes spoke to me, and I saw sadness in the dark depths of her eyes.

We talked in general terms of the mother role: about mothers, being mothers, having mothers. Lane 2 mother only called her own mother with positive news because otherwise she knew her mom would toss and turn all night long, worried about her adult daughter with children of her own. Lane 1 mother bobbed her head in agreement. You are always tied to your mother and always tied to your children was our consensus.

At the usual question, "Are you heading home or is this home?" lane 1 mother said, "Both." Since we in lane 2 both lived in Chicago, we explored this. You never know when you will find a friend, I figured. Or be a friend.

Two are better than one, because they have a
good return for their labor: If either of them
falls down, one can help the other up.

—ECCLESIASTES 4:9–10

Her parents lived in Chicago, and she frequently flew in from the coast to care for them. Her father, diagnosed only weeks earlier with pancreatic cancer, expected to live only a few more months. Her mother, broken of heart and eighty-one years old, could not navigate the challenges of her husband's health alone. And so this daughter boarded a four-hour flight as often as possible, landing at midnight, swinging into full gear to care for her parents. The dark-ringed eyes needed no other explanation.

We stood in a community of silence, bound together by the fetters of motherhood, forged at the beginning of time. Eve, the first mother, brokenhearted over the loss of two sons, lived in a world without peers and no mother of her own to share the grief and the joy, to answer her questions or offer assurance. But since then, women have circled their arms to hold their battle-weary colleagues. We three, with the many jumbled pieces of our own journeys as women and daughters and mothers rattling about in our souls, somehow formed a mosaic of mothering there at the boarding gate.

Traveling through the country, passing from one gathering to another, [Paul] gave constant encouragement, lifting their spirits and charging them with fresh hope.

—ACTS 20:2 MSG

Whatever our age, whatever our mother's age, whatever our children's ages, we mothers are always connected, regardless of how often we meet. And the pains and joys and hopes of mothering are universal: We desire the very best for our children. We long for them to live in hope and health and happiness, that they will have a means of contributing to the world. For our mothers, too, we belatedly recognize their sacrifices, the time and money and emotional wounding they endured raising us, we children who thought we deserved the moon, and our mothers trying and failing to lasso that orb for us, or boost us closer to a lunar landing.

It's not good to mother alone. It's not good to daughter alone. It's not good to be alone.

Heart Work

Sometimes a mother-daughter relationship is difficult to decode, particularly when we are younger. We simply don't have the necessary tools. Allow Psalm 34:18 to soak into your soul. Invite God's nearness as you feel your regrets regarding your own mother. Perhaps she came nowhere near lassoing the moon for you and that still hurts. Or maybe you tried to disassociate from her in ways that wounded her, and you feel shame about that. Invite God in as you feel your regrets as a parent too. Take your time. There's no hurry when it comes to building a mosaic of our brokenness.

Heart Check

What do you remember about wanting to separate from your own mother? What about her did you take for granted? If your children are old enough to feel the desire to separate from you, when and where have you seen it? How have you handled it?

Mothers speak the same language no matter our homeland. In what unlikely places have you experienced the bond of motherhood with other moms? On what occasions do you feel alone and lonely in your role?

God is near to the brokenhearted and often communicates that nearness through other mothers. Who are some of your mother friends? How might you expand your community of mothers?

Heart Cry

God,
I'm a mother,
I'm a daughter,
Caught between
Regrets
And joys,
Between questions
And certainties.
It's not good—
It's impossible—
To do this alone.
Help me to find community,
Help me to be community,

In the boarding lane
Called parenting.
Thank you that you gave
More than the moon;
You gave us yourself.

Heart of God

Dear one,
You were not designed
To function alone.
I gave you a mother,
And I made you a mother.
However disappointing
And even dysfunctional
That community may be,
It's all designed
To lead you to me
And to others
Who understand the
Joy and pain
In the boarding lane
Called life.
So find some friends,
Be a friend,
And learn how quickly
Broken hearts heal
Together.

For I have come to have much joy and comfort in your love, because
the hearts of the saints have been refreshed through you. . . .
Let me benefit from you in the Lord; refresh my heart in Christ.

—Philemon 7, 20 NASB

21

Refresh My Heart

Days after we moved to the neighborhood, she appeared at my door with her baby and stroller, a pint of fresh cherries from the farmers' market, and a gift certificate to a nearby coffee shop. Her kindness and ready laugh warmed my soul, and her initiative refreshed my heart.

For years I'd prayed for such a friend. After one move I'd had a thorough meltdown. My husband plopped down beside me and said, with compassion and honesty, "Jane, I can't be your only friend. I can't carry that weight. You need others in your life who will bless you."

Looking around at my little blessings, all three of them, I figured that wasn't what Rich meant. So I scribbled a list of the types of friends I needed: a prayer partner and accountability person, some writers because I was plunking out words on my computer with its dot matrix printer and didn't know what to do with the pages I'd created, someone in ministry to come alongside me as a pastor's wife, and a woman who was a really good mother to her children.

*One study . . . followed sixty-one women with advanced
ovarian cancer. Those with ample social support had much
lower levels of a protein linked to more aggressive types
of cancer. Having lower levels of the protein . . . also boosted
the effectiveness of chemotherapy. Women with weak
social support had levels . . . 70 percent higher in general and
two-and-a-half times higher in the area around the tumor.*[1]

As I put myself in places where I might meet friends—a Bible study, an exercise class, a small group, a writers' conference, the library—God honored those requests, bringing long-term friends into my world. This cherry-gifting friend, one of the wisest mothers ever, is also a creative living expert. She looks for life and graces the lives of those around her with flourishes of beauty and artistry. After yet another move, she showed up with a paintbrush to cover the walls in our new house. We see each other every couple of months and e-mail often. She prays for me and my family every single day. I can count on her rolling laugh and sparkling eyes and the depth of her faith. And I count myself blessed.

I also count myself healthy. Research shows that having a good friend or two is as important to good health as exercising or not smoking. Friends are good for the heart. In one study, blood pressure averaged thirty points higher in people who labeled themselves as lonely. Harvard University reports, "Heart attack survivors scoring high on tests of social isolation and stress were four times more likely to die during the three years after their attacks than those with dense social networks and little stress."[2]

Girl time increases serotonin levels, the feel-good substance lacking in people struggling with depression. Girlfriends relieve our marriage and our children of significant weight, releasing them from the impossible demands we can make when our lives lack friendships.

Many people will walk in and out of your life, but only true friends will leave footprints in your heart.

—ELEANOR ROOSEVELT[3]

Friends bring perspective and laughter and another opinion. They free us from self-centeredness and broaden our world. Without the women who have companioned me along this journey of being a woman and mother, I'm not sure who I would be or where I—or my family—would be. Friends refresh our hearts. Just what the doctor ordered.

Heart Work

As you sink into Christ's presence, thank him for his faithfulness, for all the friendship attributes you recognize in him. Just wait without hurrying. Invite God to reveal where you are lonely, to show where an empty spot needs to be filled by relationships. Linger, letting God press into your heart the types of friends you might need and where to find them.

Heart Check

Who are the friends who refresh your heart? In what areas of your life do you see a lack? Create a list of the types of friends you need in your life. Where can you look for them?

Describe what kind of a friend you are: one who refreshes others or one who lets others refresh her. Or both? Is there an imbalance? If so, how will you go about adjusting it?

Sometimes we hesitate to go deep with others because we have been wounded in the past. What hinders you from inviting people into your life for the deep heart refreshment of friendship?

Heart Cry

God,
Loneliness sneaks up on me
And I don't realize that
I'm bored or sad or exhausted
Or falling out of love
With my loved ones,
Because I have no one in my life
To come alongside me
Except you.
And you are enough for me.
But you said,
"It's not good to be alone,"
And sometimes I sure feel alone
As a woman and a mother
In this world.
I need some friends
Who will walk beside me,
Laugh with me,
Weep with me,
Drag me to my feet,
And call me forward
Into my best self.

Heart of God

Dear one,
Hear these lies
You sometimes believe:
You are alone;
You deserve to be alone;
You are better off alone.
No one has the same struggles;

No one understands.
Now how about the truth?
The statistics do not lie—
You were created for community.
It's good for your blood pressure,
But it is also good for your heart.
Refreshment,
Pouring over you,
Filling you,
Reminding you,
You are loved,
You are not alone,
You are better
Together—
You,
Me,
And some good
Refresh-your-heart friends.
I planned it just for you.

Notes

1. Tom Valeo, "Good Friends Are Good for You," WebMD, January 2007, http://www.webmd.com/balance/features/good-friends-are-good-for-you.

2. The Family Health Guide, "Making Connections Good for the Heart and Soul," Harvard Health Publications, last updated March 2007, http://www.health.harvard.edu/fhg/updates/Making-connections-good-for-the-heart-and-soul.shtml.

3. Caroline Leaper, "29 Best Friend Quotes That Sum Up Your Relationship with Your BFF Perfectly," *Marie Claire*, September 7, 2015, http://www.marieclaire.co.uk/blogs/547033/best-friend-quotes-friendship-quotes.html.

God made my life complete when I placed all the pieces before him. When I got my act together, he gave me a fresh start. Now I'm alert to God's ways; I don't take God for granted. Every day I review the ways he works; I try not to miss a trick. I feel put back together, and I'm watching my step. God rewrote the text of my life when I opened the book of my heart to his eyes.

—Psalm 18:20–24 MSG

22
Written on God's Heart

Moms of various ages sat in a small circle, many leaning forward in their chairs. At Jemma's anecdote about her child, the group roared with laughter. She laughed with them, her smile covering her whole face. "Isn't that cute? I should write it in his baby book. But he's my fourth, so he doesn't *have* a baby book."

Mothers laughed again and nodded. A first-time mom looked appalled at such poor recordkeeping. "What, no baby book?" .

"I used to ask my mom why the only things in my baby book were vaccination records," Jemma said. "But I was her fifth. At least she had a book for me."

They all laughed again. Adding children multiplies the chaos exponentially. One plus one does not equal two in the math of parenting. Keeping track of all the firsts—first smile, first tooth, first haircut—becomes a guessing game, if we even fill in those blanks, if we have the book in the first place. Parents of multiple kids need a personal scribe.

"Remember" means to re-member. To put members back together again. Re-membering leads to wholeness.

For the kids without a record of progress, it's possible to feel overlooked or neglected or like unfavored children. At least until they become parents themselves. Parenting clarifies the seeming holes in our childhood and in our parents' imperfect attempts to grow us up. Intellectually, we know that if we base our sense of self and worth on others' recorded notes about us, our lives are written on some pretty thin paper.

Maybe part of the problem is our selective recordkeeping. We keep mental track, remembering our failings and all the places where we fell apart, and the pieces of our lives—or our children's lives—feel like failed term papers. After our mothering attempts and failures, our hearts feel like wadded up balls of paper. So even if we can't put a date on them, we remember that the firsts happened—and we remember the worsts happening too.

Remember the former things, those of long ago;
I am God, and there is no other; I am God,
and there is none like me.

—Isaiah 46:9

There's hope, though, even if our parents or we ourselves aren't precise record keepers, or if the records are biased toward the bad. Because God, *God* keeps track. Psalm 139:13 tells us that God formed our inmost being, weaving us skillfully together in our mother's womb. The psalmist went on to say, "Your eyes have seen my unformed substance; and in Your book were all written the days that were ordained for me, when as yet there was not one of them" (Ps. 139:16 NASB).

God is intimately acquainted with all our ways; he knows the thoughts in our brains and the number of hairs on our heads. The Bible tells us God has a record book of our tears and even stores them in a bottle (see Ps. 56:8 NLT). For some moms, that bottle would be the size of an eyedropper, so locked up are their tears. For others, God would need an oil drum or maybe an oil tanker or an oil well.

God remembers our first smiles and our first teeth and our first words. God remembers! God can't forget. In fact, Isaiah 49:15–16 tells us that every time God looks at his hands, God remembers, "Though [your mother] may forget, I will not forget you! See, I have engraved you on the palms of my hands." Though that prophecy was first meant for the nation of Israel, we know that God remembers each one of us in the very same way. Talk about a personal scribe!

Heart Work

Sit still with your heart, that fickle and prejudiced memory keeper. Ask the Holy Spirit to remind you of your firsts, the firsts that make God smile.

Heart Check

How would you rate your heart recordkeeping: poor, nonexistent, extensive? And how about the good memories versus the bad memories; is your memory ever imbalanced? What size container would God need to hold your tears?

The heart is a tricky instrument, remembering the bad while forgetting the good. Usually we carry around a few terrible memories, either of our own mothers or of our mothering (or both). Without editing yourself, let your heart remember pivotal parenting moments. What are they, and why do you think they come to mind? Can you write a new ending to those memories, given the perspective of years?

What are some of the good things you want or need to remember? Write them in your journal so they are cemented in reality by the physical movement of your hand and by seeing the writing and hearing the words in your mind.

Heart Cry

Dear God!
I remember what I need to forget
And forget what I need to remember.
I remember the worsts
And forget the firsts.
Help me learn from my "bads,"
Receive your mercy and forgiveness,
And release those painful memories.
Please help me remember
Where, with your help,
I could put a happy sticker
On a moment
Or a day
Or an interaction
With a loved one
Or with you.
And help me learn
To live moment by moment,
Secure in the knowledge
That you have me
Tattooed on your hand.
You will never forget me.

Heart of God

Dear one,
Oh the joy
Of all those firsts:
My first look at you
In the womb,
And at your birth,
And at your first doctor's visit,
And at your first haircut,
And the list goes on and on.
Your parents are so very human,
And so are limited in their recordkeeping,
But I am keeping track,
Recording your loves, your tears,
Your firsts, your fears,
In my heavenly journal.
One day how we will rejoice
Over your days on earth.
Know that I watch over you.
I delight to share
Your delights and your difficulties.
Meanwhile, your memories
With the community of the saints
Help you remember,
Help you forget,
Help you live.

Do not forget my teaching, but let your heart keep my commandments; for length of days and years of life and peace they will add to you. Do not let kindness and truth leave you; bind them around your neck, write them on the tablet of your heart so you will find favor and good repute in the sight of God and [people].
—Proverbs 3:1–4 NASB

13
Binding Your Heart

"He's only fifteen," a mother said over coffee. "He's always loved God with his whole heart. Sometimes he's the perfect kid, and other times he lies and sneaks around. He wants freedom but isn't mature enough to use it well."

Exhaustion and worry peered from blue eyes, a peephole into her distraught heart. "I don't know what to do. Please pray for us."

Don't jump ship. Join hands. We are not alone. Motherhood is for the long haul, and only heaven unfurls the story's ending.

I wanted a magic ticket for her parenting journey. But no flying carpets come along on this white-knuckle voyage. For very few people, if any, is parenting a graceful swan dive, slipping with barely a ripple into smooth waters, then making an easy crawl stroke to the other side.

No, parenting is a belly flop from the high dive, then a choppy ride on a rudderless raft with no paddle, no provisions, no compass, no maps. The occasional shark shudders along the bow. On this sloppy, unpredictable, unmapped body of water, waves slap over the sides just often enough to keep parents wet and humbled.

Mothers of infants grip the raft with one hand, clutching their baby with the other, longing for, yet fearing, some indicator of independence—words instead of wails or walking or wearing big-kid underwear. Mothers of preschoolers crane their necks for the port of kindergarten, then feel guilty.

We know the adage "It gets worse before it gets better," something no one should quote to worn-out mothers because that is one of their great fears, and they hope and pray it's not true. The unpredictable cries and unprecedented screams and heart-puncturing desperation are more than enough for the moment. Hopefully, on a good day these are balanced by a gift: a sweet baby smile, a snuggle against your chest, innocent sleep, an adorable word.

Before it gets worse—or while we watch it happen—another sage enters, saying with a kind pat from age-spotted hands, "Enjoy this time. It goes by so fast." And we fear that to be true as well.

In no time, the diapers morph into saggy jeans and the smooth feet callus from walking then running then tearing through life. Before we blink, they're late for curfew and staying awake until four in the morning talking to a heartthrob on the phone. We don't know whether to lengthen the tether between our raft and the pier, release it completely, or bind it tight with a double bowline knot.

That day over coffee, this worried mother spoke to one woman who offered quick fixes over their lattes. I didn't. I could only share my own wish-I-would-haves. "I wish I'd paid better attention when my child cried out that way. I wish I'd listened, wish I'd done whatever it took."

*God's hand over our children far
overshadows our mistakes.*

No magic tickets. But by God's grace we can try to live without regrets. We can bind our own heart to God's, hold the mother tether with loose hands, and expect some rope burns to go with the sunburns from our raft ride.

We will reach land. And so will our child. One way or another.

Heart Work

Hold out your palms and envision the rope burns of your parenting journey. Let those hands become your petition, those wounds your wordless prayer before God. In the silence, invite Christ to bind your heart with kindness, to lash your heart to his heavenly love.

Heart Check

What happens to your heart when you hear the words, "It will get worse before it gets better"? When has someone said this to you and when were the words correct? What about, "These years go so fast"? When do you want to rush past the days, and when do you long to slow them down?

Consider your spiritual goals or hopes for your child. What are they? Where have you experienced the mother's agony of lengthening the tether between you and your child? How are you handling that change or how did you?

Which of God's words can you write on your heart to bind yourself to him and keep truth and kindness foremost in your soul?

Heart Cry

God,
I want the swan dive,
The magic carpet.
I want the kiddie rides.
I want to tether tightly
To my child
And get to the other side
Without sharks
And rope burns
And sunburns.
Instead we get a ticket
On the slow boat
With rapids and waves,
And I can't navigate
Without a compass.
But you . . .
You can walk on water.
Would you step into our boat
And tether us to you?
Still the storm in us.
Bind us to your heart,
And guide us to shore.

Heart of God

Dear one,
It's a wild ride!
Hold tightly to me;
Hold loosely to your expectations
Of your child
And of parenting in general.
Let truth and love and my Word
Guide you,
Speak to and through you.
And find yourself
Some companions in this water ride
Called motherhood.

[Speak] to one another with psalms, hymns, and songs from the Spirit. Sing and make music from your heart to the Lord, always giving thanks to God the Father for everything, in the name of our Lord Jesus Christ.

—Ephesians 5:19–20

24
Music of the Heart

Life with a seminary husband and a tiny, sweet six-month-old seemed complex enough. But along with coursework, Rich's almost-full-time job, and my part-time job, plus living with and caring for a seventy-six-year-old woman with Alzheimer's disease—well, it was a little more than my long-ignored, little-noticed, relatively young and immature heart could take. My heart started to explode.

Grandma lived in perpetual confusion, not understanding who we were, why we were there, or what had happened to her mind or her husband. As control of her memory and her life slipped from her grasp, she also lost control of her temper and snapped at me, the most consistent presence in her unmoored world.

One day, unable to make small talk or help her make sense from her confusion, I was terrified that in my own anger I might act in a way I would regret. I rummaged through her high-fidelity stereo cabinet for an album. *Oklahoma!* seemed like a happy solution to the darkness around us, with the musical's lighthearted songs and happy-ever-after ending. The farmer and the cowman could, after all, be friends. Maybe Grandma and I could too.

As the music started, I called to Grandma, "Here's something you may know! Come and listen."

She straggled into the living room, her hair wild after she'd escaped my attempts with the hairbrush that morning. As she listened to the music, a smile transformed her frightened face. She started to sing along and dance around the room.

I joined her, carrying the baby, and we formed a trio on the worn carpet, twirling to the music. Her smile never faded, neither did she forget a single word.

Music hid itself in a place in her heart separate from her fugitive memory. Long ago that melody, those words, embedded themselves in an unforgettable spot, and they reappeared at a critical time to transport her from her fear. And in the presence of the music, the explosiveness in my own heart calmed as well.

A recent study . . . randomized postsurgical critically ill intensive-care patients and had them listen to recordings of gentle Mozart piano music for one hour, during which their sedation was lifted. . . . Classical music reduced blood pressure and heart rate, lowered stress-hormone levels, and reduced the need for sedatives.[1]

Years later we brought a little band of troubadours to carol in a nursing home. A woman sat hunched over in a wheelchair, her eyes hollow, much of her meal on her chest. When we started "O Come, All Ye Faithful," her chin rose and her face brightened. She sang all the words, her voice trembling with age and emotion. She reconnected with the core of her heart and soul—and with God's heart—through the music.

No wonder a common commandment in the Scriptures is "sing." When we make a joyful noise unto the Lord (see Ps. 98:4–6), we transfer from left brain to right brain, where relationships happen, our hearts engage, and we worship. Music moves us from our list-filled, fear-flooded left brain into a sacred spot, a place where our hearts remember and redirect us to God.

The past which is not recoverable in any other way is embedded, as if in amber, in the music, and people can regain a sense of identity.

—DR. OLIVER SACKS[2]

Not unlike our physical hearts that always need to be filled with blood to pump throughout our body, our needy mother hearts crave steady filling from the presence and assurance of God. At those times, music of the heart appears from a secret storehouse to fill us and draw us back—back to our hearts, to God, and to hope. So sing out loud, all the while storing up for later.

Heart Work

Find a favorite piece of music. Let the composition roll over you and bring you into a new place emotionally and spiritually. Invite God to speak love and hope into your soul through the music.

Heart Check

When have you experienced the life-giving or mood-saving impact of music on you or your family?

How accessible is music to you? When do you choose to listen to it, and when don't you? If you aren't tech savvy and your children are, ask them if they would download some of your favorites. What are those favorites?

Consider the times when your mood typically drops or the atmosphere in your home (or car) turns sour. What music could you play to shift your heart's gears? Consider classics, hymns, and contemporary music. God tells us that Scripture never returns empty but always accomplishes the purpose it is sent for (see Isa. 55:11). Perhaps you know some Scripture set to music.[3] That is a double whammy for the heart.

Heart Cry

God!
My heart dances
With the music
That is your love,
The truth that I am loved by you.
I want to spin and twirl and collapse,
Laughing,
Into your arms,
The perfect partner,
The perfect troubadour
Who sings over me
And fills my heart
With the music of
His love.
Change my heart.
Change my mood.
Change my life.

Heart of God

Dear one,
I love that music
Speaks to you,
Fills you,
Opens you to my presence,
And heals you.
I also love that my Word says,
"Speak to one another . . . with songs."
So find some singing partners,
Sing loud,
Sing long,
Sing along.
It's all part of the whole-heart plan
For healing,
For loving,
For really living.
Go ahead;
Make some joyful noise.

Notes

1. Jessica Cerretani, "Musical Notes on Healing," Harvard Medical School, accessed February 26, 2016, https://hms.harvard.edu/news/harvard-medicine/musical-notes-healing.

2. "Music and the Brain," Music & Memory, accessed February 26, 2016, http://musicandmemory.org/music-brain-resources/music-and-the-brain/.

3. One option of this is a CD by my husband, Rich Rubietta. See JaneRubietta.com/audio.html for more information on *Quiet Places: God's Music to Restore Your Soul.*

growth

Part 5

Failure to thrive (FTT) is a diagnosable condition, usually seen in children, who, though they receive adequate care for their physical needs, don't gain weight. They don't thrive. They just survive. FTT was first identified in children who were evacuated from London during the height of the Blitz in World War II. New research has confirmed FTT in the elderly and, increasingly, in those hospitalized.

Might there be a sort of emotional FTT in some mothers who are busy raising children, tapped out emotionally and spiritually because of lack of rest, surviving on leftover nutrition by eating mostly what the kids leave behind, and having a general drive to care for the needs of others? Because of our busyness while in the thick of parenting, living waist-high in children and their friends and their schedules of activities, we might not notice this state within our own souls.

Failure to thrive . . . affects 5 to 35 percent of community-dwelling older adults, 25 to 40 percent of nursing home residents, and 50 to 60 percent of hospitalized veterans.[1]

For me, spiritual (and relational) failure to thrive showed up after my second child's birth. My family moved from a full and, yes, hectic, and, yes again, absolutely insanely over-involved life in suburbia to a country parish. The area offered new insight into the term *rural*. We had the church and a cemetery on one side of us, and on the other, our primary neighbor.

Here's a snapshot of my family at that time: two children aged two and under, a husband working double shifts pastoring two churches, and one mother hanging on by her hair and faring poorly in all her roles. Compounding the issue was the fact that I understood neither my gifts nor my natural talents and had overcommitted myself so people would like me. Maybe I figured that if they liked me, they would like Jesus. Or like my husband. Or all three.

This recipe for disaster worked out just as you'd expect. A Chernobyl-sized meltdown over an inconsequential issue forced me to seek healing. My past reached into my present with radioactive tentacles and dragged me to a reality check: get help or go down — and take my family with me. If something didn't change fast, I might have ended up needing one of those rectangular spots on the other side of the church, complete with a limestone header.

Any time your reaction outweighs its trigger,
look deeper and further back for the real issue.

When I finally realized I couldn't blame anyone else for my own disaster—although I preferred blaming over taking personal responsibility if at all possible—I got help. And in that achingly slow recovery process, I began to learn for the first time the necessity of self-care. Whether through a support group, a 12-step program, seeing a physician or counselor, learning your spiritual gifts, reading helpful books, delving into new spiritual disciplines, or other forms of soul care, mothers must do what it takes to thrive. We can't afford not to. Failure to thrive is not an option, regardless of our age.

If we wait until the kids are grown, we could lose our minds. And we will definitely lose ground in terms of our own soul growth and cause repercussions on the hearts and lives of those around us. I knew I could not afford to live bleakly for one more second. Neither could my family.

Good friend, take to heart what I'm telling you; collect my counsels and guard them with your life. Tune your ears to the world of Wisdom; set your heart on a life of Understanding. . . . If you make Insight your priority, and won't take no for an answer . . . Fear-of-GOD will be yours; you'll have come upon the Knowledge of God. And here's why: GOD gives out Wisdom free, is plainspoken in Knowledge and Understanding.

—PROVERBS 2:1–3, 5–6 MSG

But self-care is a battle. Others' needs are so much more obvious, and we are created to nurture others and to tend to their needs, which are constant. However unhealthy it might be both for them and for us, we continue to meet them beyond the point of reason.

I once met a woman who cut up her child's food at every meal—and the child was a teenager. She also cut up her husband's food. You probably don't do that. I sure don't. But there are plenty of needs

I've tasked myself with meeting long after the person in question needed to take ownership of those needs.

If you tend to resist self-care, as I did, where is that coming from? When did you begin to believe that it wasn't OK to have needs, which means, in other words, when did you decide you couldn't be a human being? If Jesus had needs (and he did: food, water, rest, time with God, and companionship), why wouldn't we have them? Jesus took the time to meet his needs, and no one can say that was a selfish move on his part.

Is refusing to take care of ourselves a form of "de-selfing," of distancing ourselves from ourselves? Not having a self?

That question bears repeating—and answering—on those days when it's too easy to care for other people and ignore our hollowness and too hard to say, "I really must invest in my own soul and growth." If we want our families to thrive, let's learn to thrive too.

Note

1. Russell G. Robertson and Marcos Montiagnini, "Geriatric Failure to Thrive," *American Family Physician*, July 15, 2004, http://www.aafp.org/afp/2004/0715/p343.html.

Now God, don't hold out on me, don't hold back your passion. Your love and truth are all that keeps me together. When troubles ganged up on me, a mob of sins past counting, I was so swamped by guilt I couldn't see my way clear. More guilt in my heart than hair on my head, so heavy the guilt that my heart gave out. . . . And me? I'm a mess. I'm nothing and have nothing: make something of me. You can do it; you've got what it takes—but God, don't put it off.

—Psalm 40:11–12, 17 MSG

25

Heart Dead

On a speaking trip to Japan, I devoted one session to the subject of busyness. Afterward, a group of women crowded over a Japanese lady laboring to shape characters on paper.

"What are you writing?" I asked, peering over her shoulder.

She held up her paper. "See these two characters? Together they make the word *busy*. But if you read them separately, they say *heart dead*."

Heart dead. Well, that causes a pause, a tiny break in the busyness. My mind races—it stays busy even when my body stops—over my own storyline, and I agree: When I am busiest, I radiate stress, unable to pay attention to the people for whom I presumably stay so busy. And the toll on the heart?

Heart dead.

As stated earlier, medical studies confirm that heart disease is a leading killer of women, and stress is a primary contributor to heart disease. Isn't busyness a leading contributor to stress?

Though weighing only eleven ounces on average,
a healthy heart pumps two thousand gallons of blood
through sixty thousand miles of blood vessels each day.[1]

Let's not be statistics. These are busy times. Mothering doesn't stop, and neither does the rest of life. But surely we can parent without ending up heart dead.

Heart dead or heart alive? It's not a trick question but rather a growing-up one. Here's another question: Why? Why do I feel I need to do this, go here, help there? I'm noticing, with a little help from my watchful husband, that the answer isn't always healthy. Often I say yes to requests because of other people's needs or wants without paying attention to an even deeper issue: I want to be needed. Who doesn't? And God seeded in our hearts the desire to nurture and to help. Complicating that desire is the fact that our hearts want to be loved and valued and valuable. That makes us vulnerable to yea-saying, which produces the wrong kind of busyness.

Search me, O God, and know my heart; try me and
know my anxious thoughts; and see if there be any
hurtful way in me, and lead me in the everlasting way.
—Psalm 139:23–24 NASB

Today, I'm giving why a try. Why did I say yes to that meeting when I'm a meeting-phobe? Guilt, anyone? I feel as if I should be involved more in the local church. Why do I push myself when I'm exhausted? Try fear: Self-employed people who don't work don't get paid. And besides, if I keep moving, I appear more valuable.

Why must I run errands today when it's hot out and I'm looking a little unkempt? How about shame? Like mail carriers, good moms deliver even when it's hot because that's what good moms do. If I don't, maybe I'm not a good mom.

Guilt, fear, shame. Talk about heart dead.

So what do we do about the un-dones that result from changing our trajectory for the moment or the day? What about the people we disappoint, those who've come to depend upon our yea-saying and may not appreciate our nay?

If we would have had heart attacks or strokes, which could occur if we're heart dead for too long, we would have easy reasons for saying no. So maybe, just maybe, asking why leads us to saying no more often, which is preventative medicine. We say no so our hearts can stay alive and say yes—to the right things.

Heart Work

As you wait in silence, listen to your heart beat its faithful, steady rhythm. Where do you feel heart dead? Perhaps you will recognize some dead tissue in your soul; perhaps not. But as you wait, ask God to help resuscitate your heart.

Heart Check

Think back over your day, week, or life, and ask yourself why you made the choices you did. What answers do you get? Are those the real answers or just the first layer?

As you experiment with why, track your own reactions to saying no. What issues make your heart beat a little harder? How do others react to your no?

How will you hold fast to a heart-alive (rather than heart-dead) plan, such as asking why and then learning to say no, not right now, or let's talk about this tomorrow?

Heart Cry

Dear God,
You are the maker of my heart,
And your heart beats for me.
For me!
Help me to live in the reality of
Your love for me
And not in my own searching
For another's love and approval
Through my own work.
My own heart misses a beat
When I consider
Not earning my keep,
But you never asked me
To run along that
Heart-dead route.
Bring me back to life;
Resuscitate my heart.
I'll wait right here
Until you do.

Heart of God

Dear one,
Enough already of heart dead.
I came to give you life,
To put the pieces of your life
Back together.
Don't fracture yourself
By busyness.
"Why?" is a simple enough question
To ask your heart.
Don't be a statistic.
You don't have to measure up
In any sense.
You can't, after all.
But you are completed by my love.
Live there
And refill there,
And then there's enough to go around
To say yes,
To say no,
To live without soul regret.
Heart dead?
No.
Heart alive.
Welcome back from the dead.

Note

1. "36 Interesting Facts About . . . The Human Heart," Random history.com, posted January 28, 2010, http://facts.randomhistory.com/human-heart-facts.html.

Into the hovels of the poor, into the dark streets where the
homeless groan, God speaks: "I've had enough; I'm on
my way to heal the ache in the heart of the wretched."

—Psalm 12:5 MSG

26

The Healing Heart

At a women's retreat, Michelle, a mother with young children,
asked me, "How can I get help for my mom?"

She relayed a story of terror, of never being sure how she'd find her
mom and in what condition. Her mother carried great psychological
trauma from her own childhood, and when she invited Christ into
her life she had considered the damage eradicated. Sometimes we
buy into a false bill of goods, believing that "God the Magician"
will work a presto-change-o fix on us. Sometimes God heals in such
a dramatic way. But not always, as Michelle witnessed from a young
age. Sometimes, perhaps often, God wants us to participate in the
healing process, use the various support avenues he provides all
around us, and do the hard work healing requires. But Michelle's mom
hadn't done this and hadn't experienced God's healing. Her mother
took everything personally, worried incessantly about what others
thought of her (always assuming that they did think of her), and was
so wounded that she would often collapse against the wall, sobbing

and clawing at her face. Michelle would pull her mother's hands away and hold them, hold her, to stop her mother from hurting herself.

***When children parent the parents, relationships
will be compromised until the adult child's
trauma is honored and healing has begun.***

Michelle described her mom as sad, lonely, afraid of other people's opinions, and certain that she wasn't measuring up. If Michelle tried to invite her to seek help or reach out, her mother flipped on her, plunging into suicidal behavior. So every day of her life since toddlerhood, Michelle carried the responsibilities of an adult, an adult on constant suicide watch over her mother.

Of course Michelle wanted to help. She loved her mother deeply and lived with sorrow and what-if fear daily. She just didn't know how to intervene.

My own heart hurt as I listened to her story. "You grew up in that level of trauma?"

She nodded. "I got married young, to escape I think. It was a mistake. He was an addict."

This made sense. Adult children of dysfunction often marry someone who recreates the atmosphere of childhood: the abandonment, the chaos, the pain. She got out of that marriage and its craziness, grew spiritually, and married a wonderful man. From that base, she wanted to help her mother.

"And what healing have you sought for your own trauma?"

"None." She paused. Her eyes filled with moisture. "I didn't think of that."

"I'm not sure how much you can help your mom at this point; but I do think you can begin to heal from that terror."

Tears showered down her face. The possibility of her own need for healing from such severe emotional and spiritual danger never crossed her mind. She'd never assessed her own heart, recognized the damage, and begun repair.

*Faith may be slippery to hold on to and difficult
to recover from for adult children of dysfunction.
But our loss of faith does not hinder God's
faithfulness or his willingness to help us heal.*

Michelle missed her own childhood, losing her heart at such a young age and being forced to live a life directed at saving her mother. And so, perhaps, in various ways have we all. We don't travel far into our own parenting journey before we recognize our brokenness of heart. And this, indeed, is a mercy: to know that we too need healing if we are to be women who offer compassion and healing to our children, our mothers, and others we encounter.

*I found myself in trouble and went looking for my Lord;
my life was an open wound that wouldn't heal. . . . I remember
God—and shake my head. I bow my head—then wring my
hands. I'm awake all night—not a wink of sleep; I can't even
say what's bothering me. I go over the days one by one,
I ponder the years gone by. I strum my lute all through
the night, wondering how to get my life together.*

—PSALM 77:2–6 MSG

Maybe healing a heart means seeing a counselor or joining a growth group or attending a 12-step program for children of dysfunction or reading up on becoming your own parent.[1] Maybe it means looking for friends who are a little further down the healing-heart trail to come alongside us in kindness and in challenge. While sometimes God heals us quickly and without effort on our own part, God usually invites us into the lifelong process of healing the heart. People who have worked hard at healing learn how to comfort others. And that, too, is part of our mother journey.

Heart Work

Listen to your heartbeat for a few moments as you sit quietly. Refuse to rush. Invite God to highlight for you the places where your heart aches. Imagine God as your parent, maybe the parent you never had, saying the words of Psalm 12:5 aloud. Say those words aloud yourself with emphasis until you begin to believe that God means it and is on the way to heal the aches in your heart. Don't worry if you have to repeat it numerous times. God is serious.

Heart Check

We think about parenting our children, and sometimes even parenting our parents, but what about parenting or reparenting ourselves? What roles did you take on as a child with your own parents? How has that impacted your heart?

What efforts have you made so far toward healing? What stops you from taking steps toward healing your heart? Why?

What practical actions could you take that would lead to healing?

Heart Cry

Oh God,
Speak into the
Bleak, dark street
Of my soul
With my heart longing
For the parenting
Only you can give.
I can't be the mother
You designed me to be
Unless I let you parent me
The way only you can.
My own parents meant well,
Just as I do,
Yet my heart still says,
"I ache."
I hear you say,
"I've had enough.
I'm on my way!"
I eagerly watch for you
And invite you into this hovel
That is my heart.
Turn this place
Into a healing heart,
Ready for company,
For you,
For my children,
For the people
You will bring my way.

Heart of God

Dear one,
I am on the way.
I've sent my Son,
Who sent the Spirit,
Who comforts you,
Counsels you,
Calls you forward.
They join you in the hovel
And the rubble
Of life on earth
And invite you into
Heart healing.
Will you say yes
So you can live,
Really live,
Lit up by the Light of the World?
Then you can sing,
"This little light of mine"
And let it shine.

Note

1. If an adult children of dysfunction group is not available, any 12-step program will offer the same principles of healing from dysfunction.

I shall run the way of Your commandments,
for You will enlarge my heart.

Psalm 119:32 NASB

27
The Enlarging Heart

She slumped in the car, twisting in the seat to make room to comfortably read her book. As daylight faded, she moved the car under a streetlight so she could see to read. Finally, this mother of two put her head against the headrest and dozed.

When the kids clambered into the car, full of excitement over art class and basketball practice, she tried to have perspective. She was happy to drive the kids to a school twenty-five miles from home, through traffic-bogged suburbs, logging one hundred miles each weekday for their entire childhood. She wanted to furnish them with every opportunity to discover their gifts and talents, and perhaps their calling. That meant more driving, more sitting in the car or cooling her jets in a coffee shop while the children experienced the joy of ballet, horseback riding, hockey, and voice lessons.

But that didn't last long. Rather than allowing her heart to lay dormant, she decided to seize these moments, these long waiting days, and reinvest in herself. So while her children took voice lessons, she enrolled in voice lessons as well with a different teacher. She learned she couldn't carry a tune alone but sang beautifully when bolstered by a group. She took dance and learned to ride horses. Her heart enlarged with every new experience.

Research shows that better-educated people tend to experience lower levels of unpleasant emotions like anxiety, anger, and depression, and fewer physical symptoms such as aches and pains.

—PAUL MARTIN[1]

Today, her children grown, she regrets nothing about the configuration of those days. Not the long commute and not the time and financial investment in the kids' activities. Because when they were growing, so was she, and she began to embrace her own gifts and interests.

How easy it is to pour ourselves into our children's growth, bringing them rich, creative experiences, while giving no thought to how we ourselves are growing and expanding. It is much simpler to sigh and forge ahead like human snowplows clearing the path for our kids than to think about who we are becoming. And not every mother is fortunate enough to be able to shuttle all day long and into the evenings. Maybe we can't afford the extra expense of lessons and classes. Some of us are strapped for time. Others work both shifts, in- and outside the home, punching a time clock and garnering a paycheck with all its accompanying stress.

But growing doesn't need to cost more money. With some ingenuity, we can fit it into our already full lives. Try audio books, and listen as you commute. Learn a language while driving. Check out free programs at the library. Start an online book club, reading the classics or books on the best-seller list. Switch genres to invigorate your mind. Watch documentaries or movies that will challenge your worldview. Home improvement stores offer free classes on everything from rewiring lamps to water gardening. Search out community college and park district offerings. Every single new experience, every growth opportunity, expands our brains and enlarges our hearts.

All the evidence that we have indicates that it is reasonable to assume in practically every human being, and certainly in almost every newborn baby, that there is an active will toward health, an impulse toward growth, or toward the actualization.

—ABRAHAM MASLOW[2]

This mother intuitively understood the words of psychologist Carl Jung: "Nothing has a stronger influence psychologically on their environment and especially on their children than the unlived life of the parent."[3] So she decided to live life every day. Rather than living life through or for her children, she lived life with her children.

Living her own life enlarged her heart, giving her a generosity of soul. This showed up as more joy in her relationships, particularly with her children, and more wisdom about boundaries for them.

And more love.

Heart Work

How big is your heart? Sit with that thought. Where is God inviting you to enlarge your heart?

Heart Check

Estimate how many hours you have spent or will spend shuttling your children to their activities, interests, and commitments. When has this been inconvenient? (Or when hasn't it?)

Self-care and personal growth can be taken to the extreme. Where is there tension between developing your own gifts and being self-centered or selfish? Describe the tension between your own growth and your mother involvement in your child's life.

What would you love to learn to do? Give yourself permission to experiment, fail, and try something else. What gifts have you shelved as you raised your kids? What one possibility can you investigate? There's no such thing as failure in this experiment— except failing to try.

Heart Cry

Really, God?
You've given me gifts and dreams
And talents and interests,
And it's OK with you
If I develop those,
Even as I try to grow as a mother,
To be the best mother possible?
My heart feels bigger already.
I feel like spinning in your arms
And spinning my child in my arms
And spinning into the woman you created me to be.
Enlarge my heart,
O God.
For your sake.
For my children's sake.
For my sake.
And for the world's sake.

Heart of God

Dear one,
When your world is too small,
Your heart may shrink to fit,
But my heart is the size
Of the world,
And I hold your heart,
And your children's hearts there.
Take a risk,
Listen to your own heart
Not just the needs of those around you.
Listen to the gifts and dreams
I planted there.
I will pour myself into you
So that you can become
All I dream for you.
I will enlarge your heart.

Notes

1. Gina Stepp, "Give Sorrow More than Words," Life & Health, *Vision*, winter 2007, http://www.vision.org/visionmedia/grief-and-loss/neuroscience/2166.aspx.
2. Ali Luke, "10 Great Quotes About Change and Growth," *The Change Blog* (blog), November 24, 2011, http://www.thechange blog.com/10-great-quotes-about-change-and-growth/.
3. Carl Jung, The Quotations Page, accessed November 29, 2015, http://www.quotationspage.com/quotes/Carl_Jung.

If [Christ's] love has made any difference in your life, if being in a community of the Spirit means anything to you, if you have a heart . . . then do me a favor: Agree with each other, love each other, be deep-spirited friends. . . . Put yourself aside, and help others get ahead. Don't be obsessed with getting your own advantage. Forget yourselves long enough to lend a helping hand.

—Philippians 2:1–4 MSG

28
Relinquish Your Heart

Her eyes almost disappear when she smiles or laughs, and she smiles and laughs easily and often. At least in public. But the smiles and laughter are hard-won. Her third child started having seizures as an infant, creating a centripetal pull for the entire household. With big sisters two and four years old, this tiny daughter's needs could easily have become a black hole for the family, spinning everyone and everything around her health issues.

Theresa couldn't have loved her children any more or any better. But some days—some days she couldn't get her bearings. Who was she? What were her gifts? Didn't she have dreams once, dreams that involved using those gifts in significant ways alongside her husband, a dynamic pastor?

And the toll on her marriage mounted. By God's grace they stayed together; by God's grace they held tightly to their vows. By God's grace they kept praying themselves and each other back to center, back to the core of their marriage, which is the heart of God.

Only by God's grace did they defy the high divorce rate for parents of special-needs children.

So now, with her daughter grown but not independent, Theresa's part-time job eats up any emotional reserves she might have had to pour back into her dreams and original calling. "This is my calling, now," she says. "Our children, our marriage, our church."

A mantra I use often, to keep me focused in delight on the person in front of me, comes from an unlikely place. I find it in Jesus' words to the good ladrón *nailed next to him. He essentially says, "This day . . . with me . . . Paradise." . . . God, right there, today, in the person in front of me, joy beyond holding, beholding this day, Paradise. You delight in what is before you today in Christ.*

—GREGORY BOYLE[1]

Maybe she didn't laugh as often as she now wishes she had. Maybe in the solace of her own house, discouragement snuck up. This wasn't the script she'd imagined for her life or her child's. She still shuttles her adult child to doctors' visits, prays and nurses her through more surgeries, and every day relinquishes her own heart to God.

Commit to the LORD whatever you do,
and he will establish your plans.

—PROVERBS 16:3

And really, is there any other way through the long days and even longer nights of this vigil called mothering? No matter the severity of our children's needs, all we can do every single day is give over to God our dreams, wishes, and sorrows—and those of our children.

One by one, we can list them and then relinquish our hearts, asking for God's timing in their fulfillment and for wisdom while we wait. Otherwise, we are likely to bury our disappointments or ignore them or maybe deny them, and they will wedge beneath the skin of our soul like a thorn, irritating and infecting.

Theresa refuses to let that happen. She hasn't forgotten those dreams and hopes, but more importantly, God hasn't either. And Theresa will wait with her heart, and God's, and continue to love. It's the only way to keep her heart.

Heart Work

Sit still, mindful of your beating heart and the complexity of the hopes and dreams you've carried with you as a mother, as a woman. What do you need to relinquish in order to live without a heart heavy from grief and loss? Open your hands and imagine offering your grief and loss to God. Now just wait. Wait for God's peace to restore your heart, one beat at a time.

Heart Check

When have you lost heart during your parenting season?

Start your own list of dreams, gifts, sorrows, and losses. Take some time to consider those items because they represent an enormous part of your heart and the burden(s) you carry around.

Consider how it might look if you relinquish your heart into God's care. Pray a relinquishment prayer for the concerns that weigh heavily on you right now.

Heart Cry

Dear God!
I have a long list of prayers,
And they mostly concern what
I want to see happen and when.
I am filled with instructions
For your care of the people I love.
And sometimes . . .
Sometimes I don't see it happening,
I don't see your plan.
And the pain?
The pain for my beloveds
Overwhelms me.
So today
I sit with my list
Of marching orders for you
And lay it down.
I relinquish my hopes,
My plans and programs,
My dreams and desires,
The instruction manual
For how our lives will work.
I open my hands
And relinquish them.
And turn to you,
Rather than to your gifts.
I will trust you,
Your timing,
Your plans,
Your hand in our lives.
For though life is hard,
Your heart is good.

Heart of God

Dear one,
You give so much as a mother.
Give,
And give up.
And those gifts carry a price tag.
You cannot grieve
What you do not acknowledge.
You cannot relinquish
What you refuse to notice.
I am your safe place,
Your refuge,
And I can hold your dreams
And your losses
And all the unexpecteds of this
Mother journey.
So bring them all to me.
We will grieve together,
And then,
Hold on to this—
I hold you
And your children
And the future,
And I have promised
Hope for all your tomorrows.

Note

1. Gregory Boyle, *Tattoos on the Heart: The Power of Boundless Compassion* (New York: Free Press, 2010), 158–159.

At about this same time [Jesus] again found himself with a
hungry crowd on his hands. He called his disciples together and said,
"This crowd is breaking my heart. They have stuck with me for three
days, and now they have nothing to eat. If I send them home hungry
they'll faint along the way—some of them have come a long distance."

—Mark 8:1–3 MSG

29

The Hungry Heart

Her heart hungered for affirmation and never found it in her husband with his perfectionistic standards. He discouraged her friendships, so she focused on home and children. As her kids grew and boarded their school buses, the hunger resurfaced. She tried to listen to her heart.

The artist within her soul peeped out, asking to be fed. She enrolled in courses after being accepted at a prestigious fine arts school. Her heart began to revive.

But finances dictated a job with a regular paycheck, and she accepted work that registered far below the graph of her heart's desires. Marriage difficulties accelerated, then, surprise! Another baby.

She hunkered down, determined to be a good mom, still working at the off-target job. Expectations accelerated, and the exit row of divorce looked better and better. Her marriage, never safe, became intolerable. She couldn't meet others' expectations, and an ugly voice said, "You can fix this. Your husband doesn't believe in you and doesn't like you as you are. You can show him. Just stop eating."

Already feeling invisible, she acted on that feeling and cut calories. She lost weight. She axed more calories, the woman in the mirror still unacceptable. She shrank. Size 0 pants slipped off her hips. She gagged on solid foods and opted for a liquid diet. The mirror smiled.

Her heart moaned, her marriage wept, her kids acted out. She wanted to disappear.

She nearly did.

> *Sit at the feast, dear Lord, break thou the bread;*
> *Fill thou the cup that brings life to the dead;*
> *That we may find in thee pardon and peace,*
> *And from all bondage win a full release. . . .*
> *Come then, O holy Christ, feed us, we pray;*
> *Touch with thy pierced hand each common day;*
> *Making this earthly life full of thy grace,*
> *Till in the home of heaven we find our place.*
>
> —MAY HOYT[1]

Her story belongs to millions of women who long for more than what marriage or family seem to offer. To be accepted and loved is the universal cry of our hearts. But at every turn, we bounce off walls of criticism and not-enoughness. Chronic shame whispers evil into our ears: "You aren't good enough. You don't measure up. You don't count."

But that woman who wanted to disappear does count. You do too. We count. Our presence matters. It's just that no one will ever love us the way we hope. Our hearts' desires will always be thwarted, leaving us hungering for more, better, different. Our parents and families and friends love us as best they can. That's the problem. Their best isn't perfect and will never be perfect. So sometimes we just want to disappear.

"I see you," God says. "I see you when you rise up, and when you lie down. Before there's a word on your tongue, I know it" (see Ps. 139:2–4). God sees. But even more, God cares. God loves and says. "I have loved you with an everlasting love" (Jer. 31:3). This love never ends, covering us even when our house is trashed or our kids disobey or we fail our husbands or they fail us.

Her battle still rages, but family rallies and friends bolster. She seeks help for her pain. It's hard to swallow the truth that she is loved, after having eaten the poison of shame for years. She may not grasp God's love yet, but God knows; God sees; God holds on. She isn't just Mrs. So-and-So, mother of multiple children. She bears God's name. And one day, her hungry heart will feast.

Heart Work

You, too, have come a long, long distance. In silence, let your heart fall open like a hungry baby bird's mouth. What is your hunger as you wait before God? Wait, not trying to fill that hunger yourself. Just wait, bringing that hunger into God's presence.

Heart Check

In what ways do you identify with the hungry heart? How does your hunger show up? In what ways do you feed it or starve it?

How much of your identity is entwined in being Ms. or Mrs. So-and-So, mother of (fill in the blank with names of your children)? Where are you on the failure graph, and who determined the coordinates on that graph?

When do you want to disappear, and how do you try to do that? What will it take to trust God enough to be seen and loved with the only perfect love? What stops you from trusting that love now?

Heart Cry

Oh God,
I'm hungry,
Hungry for more,
For better,
For different.
I want to be all those things,
But more than anything,
I hunger to be safe
And to be loved.
I want to disappear
In the mirror of my failures,
But instead they are magnified.
See me,
Find me,
Hold me,
Love me.
Do not relinquish
Your grip on me,
And please,
Feed my heart
With the truth:
My hunger breaks
Your heart,
And you have come
To feed me.
Full to the brim.

Heart of God

Dear one,
Hunger is intended
To lead you to me.
For what do you hunger?
Just naming it
Takes off the edge.
I specialize in feeding.
I am the Bread of Heaven,
The Bread of Life,
The Bread sent from heaven
To give you life.
So what are you hungry for?
It's more than food,
Bigger than affirmation,
Larger than attention.
It's perfect love,
And you can order it
Right here,
Day and night—
My specialty.

Note

1. May Hoyt, "Here at Thy Table, Lord," 1877?, public domain.

The mouth speaks what the heart is full of. A good man
brings good things out of the good stored up in him.

—Matthew 12:34–35

30

The Spilling Heart

Those aren't the words you meant to say. As soon as they hurtle
out, you want to clap your hand over your mouth. They burn your
lips on the way past and scald the hearer—perhaps one of your
children, probably someone you love, or at least, someone you want
to treat with respect. And then you want to disappear or resign for
the pain you've caused.

If you could rewind and erase the tape, you would. Where did
those wretched little bombs come from? Why did they show up now?

These people honor me with their lips,
but their hearts are far from me.

—MARK 7:6

The heart retains all sorts of information and sometimes just tips
over, spilling out diseased words or reactions. After a heart attack,

the damaged muscle dumps enzymes into the blood stream, and those enzymes become an indicator of heart attack for doctors.

Maybe our emotional heart is the same. Jesus said, "For the mouth speaks out of that which fills the heart" (Matt. 12:34 NASB). And if ugliness spills out, then our reservoir may be full of contamination or damage.

—\/❤\—

Let the words of my mouth and the meditation of my heart be acceptable in Your sight, O LORD, my rock and my Redeemer.

—PSALM 19:14 NASB

Motherhood makes us a statistic. We carry pain for our children. We cart pain for their friends or lack of friends. We haul around stress and exhaustion and loneliness. We worry about their progress on the growth charts of human normalcy and compare data with friends and their children.

And if that's not enough to create a heart full of crud, add financial problems, marriage trouble, broken stuff around the house, the anxiety of being a single mom or an older mom or a mother of a prodigal.

Under attack, our mother heart responds to the pain just as a damaged muscle in our physical heart would. The enzymes tip into our soul. From the disastrous accumulation of pain and longing, the mouth speaks or yells or whimpers or whines.

The pain that accompanies parenting can kill us and kill our souls, bit by bit. To say nothing of wounding the people we really do love.

So how about this? Write down all the stuff crammed into your heart—the good, the ugly, the unmentionable. You don't have to show this to anyone. But as my ER-nurse friend says, "Keep your feelings on the outside." This moves the toxic enzymes into a safe container bigger than your heart.

Now take the first item on the list. Is it a happy thing? Turn it into an out-loud praise. "Thank you, God. My child's test results are negative. Hallelujah." Let that praise fill the air around you and your heart too.

Maybe it's a hard subject, like anger. Turn it into a petition: "God, I don't know what to do with this anger. But I don't want it to hurt anyone else. I'm going to give it to you. Please help me deal with it. Please help me find resources to manage it."

Go through that list as many times as it takes to lighten the load. Then replace some of those items with hope, with grow words. Fill your heart with good, and the next time you open your mouth, good will spill out. Those are enzymes we can all live with.

Heart Work

Tip over your heart into God's presence, a little or a lot at a time. Let the enzymes spill into a safe holding tank—God's heart—and begin to feel your freedom. Maybe you're angry at God. Pour out your heart, God can hold your anger. After your reservoir empties, wait in silence. Now, let God's heart spill into yours: the forgiveness, the wisdom, the divine mercy that is grace.

Heart Check

When has your tongue gotten ahead of your better sense and hurt someone you love? How did you handle that then and later? What emotions showed up as a result of that verbal volley?

What fills your heart right now? Sometimes our words come from very deep wounds, inflicted long ago, because damaged hearts spill enzymes and produce disease. If that's the case for you, consider where to find healing for those wounds.

Empty hearts need to be refilled. So when you pour out, refill the space with some of Paul's remedy: "Whatever is true, whatever is noble, whatever is right, whatever is pure, whatever is lovely, whatever is admirable—if anything is excellent or praiseworthy— think about such things" (Phil. 4:8).

Heart Cry

Lord God,
Be with my mouth!
But to be with my mouth
You must be with my heart,
And that's a problem.
Please take my pain
And anger
And all the unforgiveness
I've stashed there
And the cache of resentment.
Then there's the
Mother lode of guilt.
I tip my heart over to you
Before these tip me over
And poison the people I love.
Please cleanse my heart
And fill me with yourself
So that when my mouth opens
Love falls out.

Heart of God

Dear one,
How I long to fill you with good,
To spill my love and joy
And peace and hope
And all the fruit of the Spirit
That you can hold,
To fill you full to overflowing
With goodness.
And the spillage of your heart,
The difficult words that tumbled out
Wounding others,
Allow me to help you mend relationships,
Starting with your own
Mother heart.

Wonder

Part 6

Mothers wonder about many things: if they will survive or their children will; if they will drop or break the tiny newborn; if they will be able to love a second child as much as they love the firstborn; if the laundry will ever be finished; if the teenager will remember both to make curfew and put gas in the tank. In some instances, wonder equals marveling. But in these, it is simply a soft word for worry.

Worry seems to be a common denominator for women in general and for moms of any age. My own mother, at age eighty-two, still worries when she thinks I'm tired, worries about my long drive home, and worries about my family. And I do my own daughter the favor of worrying about her and her health and family. It's basically a family legacy, this worry business.

We will never run out of opportunities to worry, and our profession is rife with every possible opportunity for the wrinkled-brow disease to appear. No doubt it's super effective for both the subject of our worry and for our own health. I wonder about research on the rewards of worry disguised as wonder—I wonder if everyone will be safe, if there will be an accident en route, if my child will ever grow up to love others.

There are so many other wonder killers in our world: exhaustion, busyness, disappointment, and plain old sin. In the Scriptures, people look to God and to God's works for wonder, and I fear we have shifted our gaze from God to gadgets. Is it possible that our smartphones have stolen our wonder?

The whole earth is filled with awe at your
wonders; where morning dawns, where
evening fades, you call forth songs of joy.
—PSALM 65:8

We often fail to see other human beings at the same table in the same restaurant with us because we are engrossed in the wonder of our phones. We fail to look into others' eyes, to be lost in wonder at the depth of their loving look at us or the depth or real meaning of their questions or their hope or pain.

Our technological wonders have not done wonders for our brains. Research indicates an alarming decrease in attention span and memory. Piaget's theory of cognitive development outlined the process of acquiring knowledge, assimilating it and then putting it into practice.[1] Jean Piaget recognized that human intelligence develops through physical play, something children being raised with a phones and tablets in their hands and televisions and computers in their bedrooms experience less and less frequently. I wonder what effect technology has had on our adult wonder levels?

This mental process of awareness, perception, reasoning, and judgment can only be built if the child experiences something physical, like playing with clay, blocks, or a bat and ball. It isn't possible if [he or she] is staring into a screen and conquering angry birds.

—Shraddha Shah[2]

If physical play develops a child's cognitive understanding, movement also helps us integrate our bodies with our souls. And it helps develop genuine "wonder-lust." And wonder lasts.

The pumping of the human heart sends oxygen to the lungs, dumping off oxygen and picking up carbon dioxide in a simultaneous gas exchange. Wonder does for the soul what those hardworking involuntary organs do for the body; wonder oxygenates our hearts.

We can't begin to estimate the benefits of wonder, of noticing the miraculous moments—and the marvelous timings that can be attributed only to God's kind hand in our lives. Imagine the benefits of breathing in the wonder, of paying attention and letting the oxygenation of wonder create its own rush in the bloodstream and brain. It's like a spa for the heart and soul, except it's free.

We fail to wonder because we lack the attention span to notice the awe-inspiring. Commitments jam our lives and our schedules in those heavy parenting years. Responsibility renders us wonder blind rather than blinded by wonder.

The wonder is not that we fail, mess up, drop balls, and cross wires. The wonder is that in spite of those little and big issues we are so deeply loved. Wonder is that wide-open heart space of

Psalm 18:19: "He brought me out into a spacious place; he rescued me because he delighted in me."

Wonder is about big moments and milestones as well as tiny wonder bursts of freedom and joy. Wonder invites us away from the worry and redirects our gaze to the miracles that fill our days and nights, pouring color in- and outside the lines of our lives.

Wonder may help us live longer.

And it will definitely, absolutely, help us live better and brighter and love bigger. It's like vitamin D, sunshine for our colorless souls.

Notes

1. *Wikipedia*, s.v. "Piaget's Theory of Cognitive Development," last modified February 24, 2016, https://en.wikipedia.org/wiki/Piaget%27s_theory_of_cognitive_development.

2. Reema Gehi, "Your Smartphone Is Destroying Your Memory," *The Times of India*, December 3, 2013, http://timesofindia.indiatimes.com/life-style/health-fitness/health-news/Your-smartphone-is-destroying-your-memory/articleshow/19412724.cms.

A deep, reverential fear settled over the neighborhood, and in
all that Judean hill country people talked about nothing else.
Everyone who heard about it took it to heart, wondering, "What
will become of this child? Clearly, God has his hand in this."

—Luke 1:65–66 MSG

31
Heart of Wonder

I wonder if back when we were born our parents looked at us—
red, wrinkled, frowning, screaming babies, shriveled and traumatized
from the rude and painful exit from our mother's warm womb—and
said with hearts spilling with wonder, "Oh, what a blessing your life
will be! What a difference you already make, little one, in a calloused
and hopeless world. You bring innocence and hope. You bring great
gifts and sensitivities."

I wonder. Have pregnancy and birth always seemed as miraculous
to others as they did to us when we announced with a trill of wonder
and a tinge of fear, "We're expecting! We're going to be parents!"?
Did our parents greet our birth with bright-eyed optimism and say,
"Maybe you're the next Monet or Jonas Salk or Annie Sullivan or
Mother Teresa"?

Since the time of Adam and Eve, babies have been born and parents
have gazed at them, starstruck with wonder at this godlike happening
between two people. A life created.

*For you created my inmost being; you knit me
together in my mother's womb. I praise you because
I am fearfully and wonderfully made; your works
are wonderful, I know that full well.*

—PSALM 139:13–14

But what if every new mommy and daddy wept at the wild wonder of that infant, so fresh from God, so fresh from the mama's womb? What if every parent knew that the baby pushed into this world immediately changed everything about the world? For whether or not that baby grows into a famous personality, every baby changes the world.

Your birth changed the world. It will never be the same again because you are. You came, and your presence makes a difference. No one exists like you, with your gifts and talents, your fingerprints and scent, your sparkling eyes and way of loving. Your DNA punctured the toughened skin of this long-spinning world, adding meaning to its existence.

So you've never won an award or invented correction fluid or flown the Atlantic or juggled home, family, a paycheck, and a hundred committees at church. Even if you've never done more than volunteer at school or carpool kids or put meals on the table or none of the above or all the above but poorly, even if your sole contribution to this world is the fact of your birth, it is a wonder.

Like Jimmy Stewart in *It's a Wonderful Life*, imagine the people who would not have been touched by your hand, loved by your touch, handed the gift of life by your presence. And even though you haven't always done life well, even though (not *if*) you've made mistakes and misspoken and misacted, you exist. Therefore you have meaning; your life has meaning.

*There is no way of telling people that they are
all walking around shining like the sun.*

—THOMAS MERTON[1]

Whether you've forgotten that truth or life's wounds wiped it clean from your memory, or whether your parents ever thought, let alone voiced, such a heart of wonder or felt that kind of blessing is irrelevant. Even if you don't feel as though you were born under the blessed banner of wonder, you really were.

And God has never gotten over the wonder of you.

Heart Work

Go before God and ask about that wonder statement. Invite God to show you the times when you haven't felt like a wonder and to communicate that wonder to you. Take time to just . . . wonder.

Heart Check

Do you feel guilty about what you may have communicated to your child, who, frankly, behaves as less than a wonder sometimes? In what ways can you hang that banner of blessing over your home that reads, "You Are a Wonder"?

Where and when have you sensed that your life is a wonder? From whom? In what instances have you lacked that sense of wonder?

What difference does it make to you to know you're a wonder? Do you find that hard to believe? How can you move into a place where you feel its truth?

Heart Cry

Oh, God,
I don't think the stars sang
And the world wondered
When I was born.
I'm not John the Baptist or Teresa of Avila,
And I'm not even a very good version of myself.
To be honest,
I find it hard to believe
That I am a wonder.
And I wonder sometimes
Why you created me
And whether I am a mistake,
And it's hard to see where my touch,
My life,
My DNA
Makes a difference in this world.
And my heart is deafened
By the cries in the world
And the mistakes I've made
And my failures at loving.
But I refuse to believe the lie
That the world is better without me,
And I turn to you.
Help me hear the truth:
You created me,
Therefore I am.
And I am a wonder,
Created for wonder,
Created for wonderful, new ways
Of loving and living.
The old is gone
And the new is come
And I am a wonder.

Heart of God

Dear one,
You are a wonder.
Say it with me,
"I am fearfully and wonderfully made."
May your soul know it very well.
Ask me to help you
Recognize your wonder,
Because your birth
Changed the world
For the better.
You bring hope;
You bring life;
You bring promise.
Don't believe the old, ugly lies.
Believe me when I tell you
The heavens sang
The day of your birth.
And if you listen,
The stars still sing over you,
And so do I.
I'm glad you were born.
I'm glad you are here.
I'm glad you are mine.

Note

1. Thomas Merton, *Conjectures of a Guilty Bystander* (New York: Doubleday Religion, 1966), 155.

Moreover, when God gives someone wealth and possessions,
and the ability to enjoy them, to accept their lot and be happy in their toil—
this is a gift of God. They seldom reflect on the days of their life,
because God keeps them occupied with gladness of heart.

—Ecclesiastes 5:19–20

31

The Glad Heart

Daily she awakened with thoughts of the busy schedule looming ahead and the little kids who dotted the landscape of her life. Although she had no such thing as spare time, or anything remotely resembling quiet time, Nora loved to serve her young family. Her gifts of organization and administration synced beautifully with her listening skills, enabling her to spend a moment in reflection before she jumped into the fray. She created a calm, happy environment in her home as she concentrated on her growing kids and hardworking husband.

But as the years wore on, her heart became less and less glad. Joy diminished. Love became work.

Anxiety in [one's] heart weighs it down,
but a good word makes it glad.

—PROVERBS 12:25 NASB

Then, one summer morning just before her teens awakened, her soul already feeling cramped for space, Nora remembered her Bible study from the previous school year. During the closing session, women had taken turns mentioning Scriptures through which God had spoken to them during their nine months together.

As each woman had shared and at hearing God's Word, Nora's heart had tumbled about within her in joy, like a kid at gymnastics class. She had flipped open her notebook and, in her floral artist's script, recorded all the Scripture references.

So on this dim, dull, heart-crowded day, Nora pulled out her notebook and looked up each reference in her Bible. She decided to take one little verse or section that day and read it over and over until it sank into her soul. That morning, she read Isaiah 66:13–14: "'As one whom his mother comforts, so I will comfort you; and you will be comforted in Jerusalem.' Then you will see this, and your heart will be glad, and your bones will flourish like the new grass; and the hand of the LORD will be made known to His servants" (NASB).

Her heart turned over and over, somersaulting at the thought of God showing his hand in her life. The truth that God loved her enough to display that care and provide that guidance moved her back to God's heart. She resolved to watch for God's care, then packed up her errand bags and headed out the door. At the farmers' market, she happened onto someone belonging to an artists' guild, a group that could connect her to art shows where she might display her oil paintings. She didn't like marketing, didn't know this woman, and had never heard of the guild. What were the chances of meeting her there? Her heart was glad. This opened the door for a showing, which would win her an award. And her heart was glad.

And then on her night watch, that middle of the night time when our children's situations trouble and worry and confound us, Nora wondered about her son being placed in what he called "math for dummies." She worried that he'd be relegated to low-income work for the rest of his life. But the witness of God's hand and of his comfort rose from a surprising source. The next day, her daughter mentioned that half of her friends had taken the class and, "Really, Mom, it will be fine for him."

And her heart was glad.

None of these examples are world-shattering, headline news. But isn't that how God comes to us, in subtle ways, inviting us into the comfort only he offers? And isn't that alone enough to make our hearts glad on this often perilous, usually uncertain, sometimes tedious, generally crowded, occasionally dull journey of parenting? God sees us; we can see God's hand; God cares enough about us to make that hand known to us—well, it blesses our bones. Our hearts are, indeed, glad.

Heart Work

Let's be honest. Our hearts aren't always glad. We don't always enjoy our toil in this vast wilderness of parenting. Hold that thought, and bid God to reveal those places, both dull and dark, that steal the gladness from your heart. The journey through to joy and gladness of heart grinds to a halt when we don't pay attention, either to the dull and dark times or to God's hand at work. As you wait, may God's hand appear in kindness, in love, and in blessing. Keep waiting, perhaps with your own hand over your heart as a promise and a benediction.

Heart Check

What darkens the sunrise of your day? When are you most susceptible to soul crowding and the shadows it throws on the walls of your heart?

In what circumstances does joy diminish for you and love become work? In what ways, both negative and positive, have you handled that?

Perhaps your wealth isn't in silver and gold or stocks and bonds, but rather in rich experiences and intersections, when God enters into our ordinary world. Share some instances of spotting God's glad hand and ways you keep on the lookout.

Heart Cry

Well, God,
Who knew this could ever,
Or occasionally,
Or frequently,
Be a season of dull and dark
And no gladness of heart?
But today, I choose to look
For the flash of your hand
Surprising me
In the world around me,
In the words of people I love,
In the unexpected gifts
In this toiling way
Called parenting.
That you care enough to show your hand
Makes my heart flip-flop,
And even if I don't see your hand
Today or even tomorrow,
I will look to you,
And my heart will be glad
Because you are present
Even in—
Especially in—
The invisible times
Of dull and dark.

Heart of God

Dear one,
Watch for my hand,
Watch for wonder,
Watch for joy,
Watch for those precious intersections
That you couldn't design
But I can coordinate.
I long for you to find goodness
In your day,
For my love and care
To take away the dull and dark
So that you might be
Occupied with gladness of heart.
After all,
Glad is good for your
Mother heart.

I, Jude, am a slave to Jesus Christ . . . writing to those loved by God the Father, called and kept safe by Jesus Christ. Relax, everything's going to be all right; rest, everything's coming together; open your hearts, love is on the way!

—Jude 1–2 MSG

33
The Open Heart

For the first fifty-seven years of her life, Jenni guarded her heart in the way a warden guards prisoners—with lock and key. Her mother's criticism told her, "You must be perfect. You must behave. You must make me look good." But even as Jenni guarded her heart, protecting herself from that poison, she knew she needed to love. As she opened her heart to Christ, he opened her heart to adoption. She adopted a five-year-old with Down syndrome and became Amanda's fiercest advocate and protector. Though Jenni continued to guard her own heart as a protection against her mother's lifelong disapproval, loving Amanda began to heal her own child heart.

But a special-needs child requires special attention, and Jenni's advocacy for her daughter took precedence over every other detail. A bevy of hard-to-find and even harder-to-retain helpers required constant juggling. Keeping a steady-paying job was nearly impossible due to her daughter's care, so financial problems plagued them. Health issues multiplied for Amanda, and surgeries and doctor visits were traumatic. Jenni's own needs often occupied the backseat, as did her gifts and dreams.

The centripetal pull on Jenni's life, in spite of her own mother's imprisoning presence, has been her daughter. Amanda has centered Jenni, reminding her of simple joy as her daughter sang praise songs from an in-home hospital bed. Amanda reminded her mother of simple truth and rich faith, memorizing bits of Scripture and declaring herself a princess because God is both her King and Daddy. Amanda lived with a flesh-and-blood mother who loved her and showered her with that love in practical and whimsical ways. And she lived under the sheltering wingspan of her heavenly Daddy.

While research on the neurological effects of music therapy is in its infancy, what is known is that a number of regions in the brain are activated by listening to music. And scientists say the brain responds to music by creating new pathways around damaged areas.[1]

But for Jenni, keeping her heart open wasn't only about loving Amanda. As a single mother of an adopted, special-needs child, Jenni received plenty of disapproval and even condemnation about her situation from presumably well-meaning people. To counteract those voices that echoed her own mother's voice, Jenni sought ways to keep her heart open. She says, "A critical part of my being able to both guard my heart and keep an open heart has been the rare friend who has respected me."

Young Amanda's faith inspired Jenni, who played praise music in their home and memorized Scriptures, bolstering their relationship with God and lightening her exhaustion. Jenni initiated a prayer team to cover her tiny family in prayer, and she tried to live only in the present moment. Anxiety about the next days or months or years could swallow her soul, so she tried not to project into the future, realizing Jesus' words in Matthew 6:34 were meant to calm her heart and guard her in a good way: "Therefore do not worry about tomorrow, for tomorrow will worry about itself. Each day has enough trouble of its own."

Jenni's story reminds us that keeping our hearts open requires tending to our souls' critical needs. Otherwise, we attempt to give good things to our children from empty pockets. We choose daily whether to focus on and be imprisoned by the dour people who inevitably appear with dismal predictions and discouraging words or to focus on God's promises and presence in the midst of difficult, complicated, and sometimes painful situations.

Today, Amanda is thirty years old, and her faith in her Jesus burns brighter than ever. And Jenni? Jenni is a laughing, exultant warrior, made strong by God's love, her heart always open to the God who provides. With an open heart, she has been able to see and participate in the most dynamic example of unconditional love.

And the lesson of the open heart? Perhaps it is this: "And a little child will lead them" (Isa. 11:6).

Heart Work

Given the keen competition for our time and attention, keeping an open heart is difficult. Try imagining your heart as a gate, and invite Jesus to swing open the gate of your heart to his presence. Invite him to raise your awareness of the places your heart is overly guarded and the reasons why. Rest there. Love is on the way.

Heart Check

What does it mean to you to be called and kept safe by Jesus Christ? When and where have you experienced that? Whose critical voices do you hear, either currently or echoing from your past? How can you relax in the truth that you are kept safe by Christ?

Describe the messages you've heard, received, and believed about your inadequacies, your failures, or how disappointing you are to someone. Now focus on what God says about you.

Who supports you in your parenting efforts? If you have a special-needs child, in what ways might you seek extra fortification? Where have you found your heart opened by your child's loving presence and unconditional love or by his or her untainted faith in both you and God?

Heart Cry

Oh God,
How I long for this to be true,
To know that your love is on the way,
To be able to relax into this day
And know that even the problems
Cower under the umbrella of your
Love and protection of my child
And of me.
Please keep my heart open,
Open to your presence
In the present moment
Through my child,
Through the difficulties,
And even through the negative voices I hear,
And sometimes even my own negative voice
With its tone of disapproval and judgment.
Help me hear the truth:
I am loved by you,

Called by you,
Kept safe by you.
Everything's coming together.
Everything's going to be all right.
Your love
Is on the way.
Please, come quickly.

Heart of God

Dear one,
Relaxing and parenting seem like oxymorons
In the journey of mothering
And of tending your own soul.
The needs are enormous;
The stress is overwhelming;
The joy is magnanimous;
The rewards are unimaginable.
But listen,
You are called,
You are kept safe;
Everything's going to be OK.
Because love is on the way.
Love is here to stay,
Today
And tomorrow
And always.
So please,
Relax.

Note

1. Spencer Michels, "The Healing Power of Music," PBS Newshour, February 27, 2012, http://www.pbs.org/newshour/bb/health-jan-june12-musictherapy_02-27/.

Come out, and look, you daughters of Zion. Look on King Solomon
wearing a crown . . . on the day of his wedding, the day his heart
rejoiced. . . . "You have stolen my heart, my sister, my bride;
you have stolen my heart with one glance of your eyes."

—Song of Songs 3:11; 4:9

34
Stolen My Heart

Long before her birth, our daughter stole our hearts. And when she was born, one glance at this miniature miracle, with eyes so big and expressive, like portholes into the mysteries of heaven, and our hearts were forever gone. My husband and I prayed for her, rocked her, and sang over her. And when her brothers came to join the family, they, too, stole our hearts. At each birth, a single, hot tear tracked my Rich's cheek, forever branding him as a father.

So we cuddled and prayed and laughed and steered and danced. We loved these babies, wanting the best for them all their days. From their birth, we prayed for their spouses, that God would prepare the perfect mate for the perfect time for each of them.

And God prepared and plotted, and along came the man who would woo and win our daughter's heart.

The day before the wedding, with all the frenzy of creating bouquets and packing my daughter's room and tending to multiple lists and details, we raced for one final fitting of the bridal gown.

My heart slipped away from me, seeing this young woman standing tense but beautiful beyond belief. I breathed deeply. We adjusted jewelry and veil, pinched seams. Perfect, just perfect.

She swept into the changing room, this almost-bride daughter of ours, this daughter of God's heart, and reemerged as Ruthie. Just Ruthie, precious child-turned-adult, but always our little girl.

The morning of the wedding, the air crackled with anticipation. Our daughter stayed put while I ran for the freshly pressed dress. It filled the backseat of our borrowed Jeep, full and luxurious, a mountain of fabric.

Feeling as if I carried the crown jewels, I called my almost-son. My voice trembled. "Honey, it's your almost-mom. Guess what's in my car?"

He couldn't guess.

"Ruthie's wedding dress." I paused then swallowed hard. "I guess this makes it official."

He laughed, exultant, a joyful waterfall through the cell phone.

And the wedding . . . oh, the wedding! Full of drama and laughter and joy and beauty and flowers and complications and lovely music and candlelight. Full of family and friends who love this couple deeply.

For right now, until that completeness, we have three
things to do to lead us toward that consummation:
Trust steadily in God, hope unswervingly, love
extravagantly. And the best of the three is love.

—1 Corinthians 13:13 MSG

Many people cry at weddings. But as I turned and saw our child, I gasped and nearly sobbed. Her daddy's eyes reddened, though he still insists he wasn't crying as he led her down the aisle. Tears slid down my father-in-law's cheeks without shame.

The bride moved toward the groom, her face a candle lit from within. All our mistakes, sorrows, and regrets slipped away as we saw the result of all those years of God's faithfulness.

At the reception, our new son said, "When Ruthie entered the sanctuary, I almost lost it. One look, and I was a goner."

She had stolen his heart with one glance.

Ah, the joy of a wedding, the celebration of being truly loved forevermore.

And isn't that the story we glide into every day? For we, too, are brides, whether married now or not.

The Revelation given to John says, "Hallelujah! For our Lord God Almighty reigns. Let us rejoice and be glad and give him glory! For the wedding of the Lamb has come, and his bride has made herself ready. Fine linen, bright and clean, was given her to wear" (Rev. 19:6–8). We are Christ's bride. He looks at us with delight and joy, compassion and forgiveness.

And every day, we get to live as though we are going to a wedding. Our own.

Because we are.

Heart Work

Be still with your heart and soul. Of course there are regrets and sorrows, guilt and fear. But wait now. The One who loves you forevermore wants to meet your gaze. Listen. Listen! Do you hear him say, "One look, and I was a goner"? Wait until you hear, deep in your heart, Christ's love for you.

Heart Check

How did your child steal your heart? When did you notice it was missing?

Find a wedding picture, your own or a loved one's. Recall the emotions, the intensity of that day, the charge given to the bride and groom, the hope of all that was to come. When do you experience this kind of reaction with God?

What would it be like to live every day in anticipation of going to your own wedding? How would that affect your behavior, your attitude, your heart? How can you begin to live in that anticipation?

Heart Cry

Dear God,
I stand at the door
To the sanctuary of your heart
And meet your gaze.
Your love steals my breath;
My heart thuds in response.
You love me.
Teach me how to love you well.
Teach me how to live every day
Anticipating the moment
When we meet face-to-face.
And your heart tips over into mine,
Filling me with that forever love.
While I wait here,
Show me how to love.
And to live in the wonder that
You love me.

Heart of God

Dear one,
You've stolen my heart
With just one glance.
I knew you before you were born.
I have loved you
Since eternity past,
And while we wait
For that great wedding feast in heaven,
Let me show you my love.
Watch for it
In the gifts of the day,
The beauties along the way,
The way the sun shines through tears,
The way the moon reflects the sun.
All are prisms of my love
For you,
The wonder
Of being fully loved.
Live out that love every day
Until we meet face-to-face.
I can't wait to see your smile.

How long, LORD? Will you forget me forever? How long
will you hide your face from me? How long must I wrestle with my
thoughts and day after day have sorrow in my heart? . . . Look on me and
answer, LORD my God. Give light to my eyes, or I will sleep in death. . . .
But I trust in your unfailing love; my heart rejoices in your salvation.
I will sing the LORD's praise, for he has been good to me.

—Psalm 13:1–3, 5–6

35
Sweetheart

The winter days closed around me like a collapsing snow fort,
and I knew I had to either go build my own igloo so my family
wouldn't disown me or just ride off into the sunset. Somehow.

Then my daughter called and said in her happy, chirping voice,
"Mom! I'll be out of town for a week. Would you like to use my
apartment for a writing retreat?" My heart flip-flopped like a small,
delighted child turning somersaults of happiness.

*Praise be to the LORD, for he showed
me the wonders of his love.*

—PSALM 31:21

Getting to the apartment required a one-hour train ride on the
morning commuter then a forty-five-minute walk, unless I jumped
on a bus. I cleared the new plan for my Tuesday through Thursday

soul retreat with my husband (did I detect relief in his eyes?) and our at-home high-schooler, choosing to leave my laptop at home so I wouldn't be tempted to work. After throwing a minimal amount of clothes and food into my overnight suitcase, I scribbled a few instructions.

Rich appeared with a smile and bowed, "Your chariot awaits."

He dropped me off at the train station. "We'll be fine, Jane. You need this. Have a great time." I fretted about the schedule and the trickiness of raising a teenager. Rich hugged me. "I can handle everything."

When I climbed onto the train, relief flooded me with enough adrenaline to push through my exhaustion and the slush and snow until reaching the shoebox-sized apartment in Chicago.

I lugged my bags up four flights of stairs, opened multiple locks, and plopped into my daughter's home. My heart responded with an enormous sigh, as though to say, "Finally. You are taking care of me now."

I slept. I read. I journaled. I prayed. I walked. I slept some more. Only the needs of my heart dictated the agenda. I wanted to connect with God in depth and breadth, in ways that the normal, crowded noise of daily life prohibited. I wanted to hear God's voice again.

More than anything, I wanted to know God loved me. Still. And loved me anyway, and in spite of . . . everything.

There is a longing in us all to be God-enthralled.
So enthralled that to those hunkered down in their disgrace,
in the shadow of death, we become transparent messengers
of God's own tender mercy. We want to be seized by that
same tenderness; we want to bear the largeness of God.

—Gregory Boyle[1]

I wanted to know he loved me in spite of my faults, my ear deaf to the Holy Spirit's wooing, my neglect of our love relationship. In spite of long work hours and the debris of failure that piles up in heart and soul forming a wall of rubbish that separates me from God and others. In spite of my distractions, and the if-only regrets so constant when mothers face their families and see the fallout of mother imperfection.

On Thursday, my last morning, I stretched out on the bed, reluctant to get up, change the sheets, and prepare for reentry to the life I'd left behind. The longing in my heart for a significant encounter with God still ran beneath my thoughts in a whisper. I really wanted to feel God's love for me, not just know or read or write or think about it.

The red power light of the stereo stared from across the room like a cyclops's eye. Maybe music would form a nice ending to this time. Pressing the play button started a laborious shuffling within the system, some mystical internal process, until at last the sorting mechanism landed on one of many discs within. And into the room crooned Bing Crosby's voice and a melody I hadn't heard in years: "Let me call you sweetheart; I'm in love . . . with . . . you."[2]

The words poured over me in blessing and my heart leapt.

I rarely play music and even more rarely in someone else's home. I had no idea why Bing rested in my daughter's stereo. What were the odds that all that shuffling would lead to the one song that was a direct hit for my deepest longing?

For the rest of the day, my heart twirled like a ballerina, the tune and words floating over and in me. On that note, I could return home, loved, and ready to love again.

Heart Work

Wait with your regrets and longings. Wait with your hopes. Now, place your hand over your heart and close your eyes. Feel the rhythm beneath your palm. Just wait there. Tune in, feeling the miracle of a pumping heart. After all these years and all the joys and mistakes, your heart still beats. Your life goes on. Invite God to be present. Open your heart to your longings for heavenly love. Wait for God's love to begin to beat in you. You are loved. You are God's sweetheart. God is crazy about you. Listen, do you hear it? It's that faint love song: "I'm in love . . . with . . . you."

Heart Check

Where and when do you best experience God's love and presence? How and when will you get yourself to that place? Is there anything about God's love for you that you find hard to believe? Why?

What regrets get in the way of feeling God's love for you? Of feeling God's forgiveness?

Look back over your season of motherhood, however many years that may be. Where are the places God showed up, loving you?

Heart Cry

Can it be true, Lord?
You still love me?
You really, really love me?
All the "in spite ofs" crowd my brain
And tell me your love is a lie.
Because I have failed.
I have a history of not being a perfect mother.
Though I fail,
Your Word says

Your love is unfailing.
So I choose to put my failures and regrets,
My imperfections and broken dreams
For myself and my family,
Into your hands
And believe the truth—
You love me.
You really, really love me.
And my own child heart leaps and twirls.
I bask in your smile.
You love me.
You really, really love me.
Let me hear you sing
Your love song over me
All the days of my life.

Heart of God

Dear one,
Let me call you sweetheart
All the day long,
All the days of your life.
My love for you is unrelated
To your performance,
To your perfections,
To your imperfections,
To how your children turned out
Or who they will become
Or what they make of their lives.
I created you.
You are my workmanship,
The art of my heart,
And I love the art I create.
You are my sweetheart,
The sweetness of my heart.
Do you hear me singing over you?

Notes

1. Gregory Boyle, *Tattoos on the Heart: The Power of Boundless Compassion* (New York: Free Press, 2010), 44–45.

2. "Bing Crosby—Let Me Call You Sweetheart (1934)," YouTube video, posted by "CatsPjamas1," April 4, 2011, https://www.youtube.com/watch?v=GgvDariuAN0.

Hallelujah! Thank GOD! Pray to him by name! Tell everyone you meet
what he has done! Sing him songs, belt out hymns, translate his wonders
into music! Honor his holy name with Hallelujahs, you who seek GOD.
Live a happy life! . . . Remember this! He led his people out singing
for joy; his chosen people marched, singing their hearts out!

—Psalm 105:1–3, 43 MSG

36
A Heart Full

As Rich and I visit with our daughter and her brand new
husband in their home, we look at happy honeymoon pictures and
see the newlyweds together in their home for the first time—cheerful,
married, laughing, teasing—their strengths complementing one
another.

They rustle up a hearty breakfast, and we feast on the joy and their
presence. Then we load the car and, realizing we're late to church,
rush through a stoplight threatening to turn an incriminating red.

We meet their friends outside the church. Now we really are late
and wait outside the sanctuary, hushed and expectant along with
other latecomers.

When the doors swing open, Rich and I follow the kids up the
side aisle to the front row. My beloved and I had shed most of our
belongings, leaving all but my small clutch in the car with our
luggage, ready for the flight home. And I realize we left our reading
glasses tucked in the baggage, so we can't read the miniature bulletin

font or the unfamiliar words or notes to the hymns. The kids sing with gusto and reverence. Rich and I smile at one another, edging a little closer to hear their harmonies. My heart twitters in my chest. Still we can't catch the tune or the meter. In fact, there is no meter on the left margin of the staffs.

We throw open our doors to God and discover at the same moment that he has already thrown open his door to us. We find ourselves standing where we always hoped we might stand—out in the wide open spaces of God's grace and glory, standing tall and shouting our praise.

—ROMANS 5:2 MSG

How replete I am, sandwiched between my husband and daughter in the front pew at church, something we rarely, if ever, experienced when the children were growing up, with their daddy up front in the pulpit while we raced up the side aisle to slide into the front pew, a mother and her gaggle of children.

I turn my head toward this man I love. Rich grimaces, squinting to read the hymn lyrics. Despite his musician's gifts, the melody and words elude him. He whispers, "Mr. Bean goes to church," then turns bug-eyed and goofy, making operatic shapes with his mouth to imitate the British movie character.

A laugh escapes me, and I close my mouth to choke down more laughter, but my body shakes as he sings big, round, wordless notes a split second after the organ. I convulse, finally burying my face entirely into Rich's shoulder so our adult kids don't have to separate their parents in church.

Rich mimes more round sounds, all sincere and deep measures of praise. I actually snort into his neck! I am helpless with joy and laughter, my daughter and her husband on one side, my own husband on the other. And over and around me, sounds of praise pouring from the pipes and rolling over the ceiling.

I am God's child, and I am loved. God is good, and life is hard. Life is good, and God is good. And the entire journey is worth the steep price of admission, everything leading up to this moment, all the memories and pain and joy and sadness and mistakes and healing and hope. All of it. Every note of it, with no meter and no measure and no key signature. And no glasses.

I wipe away tears of laughter and squeeze my husband's arm. The song ends. We sit, lock-shouldered, a foursome, and continue in worship.

My heart, my heart is filled to overflowing.

Heart Work

Gauge the state of your heart right now. Full? Empty? Happy? Sad? Wait with that. Now imagine yourself running down the side aisle at church, sliding into the front pew, late but happy, with Jesus on one side, your children on the other. Jesus sings to you, round wordless notes, and you dissolve in laughter into his neck. And you are loved. You are loved.

Heart Check

When and how do you experience the laughter that leads you to God's heart?

By what means does God refill your heart? Is it through music, Scripture, silence, beauty, movement?

When and where have you seen the mistakes and wrong notes of your mother journey turn into music?

Heart Cry

Dear God,
I see you smile
At our delight
In one another
In your house,
In your presence.
Thank you
For redeeming the years,
For your goodness,
For your love,
For your joy,
For your forgiveness,
For the little ones you loan us,
For your goodness to them,
For the hope
That this meterless mothering
Will create notes
And words
And a tune
One day,
A melody rich and round,
Poured out,
Filling my heart,
Filling the world.

Heart of God

Dear one,
No notes,
No meter,
But a heavenly rhythm
Pulsing out my love for you,
Translating my love
Into life and laughter.
You are the joy of my heart,
The great wonder of the world.
I love you with all my heart
And will spend the rest of your life
Showing you,
Singing to you,
Rejoicing over you.
Sing out hymns!
Belt out music!
Translate my wonder
Into joy and love
As you live your life
Loving your family
Toward me.
Life is hard,
Mothering is hard,
But I am good,
I am faithful,
And together we change
The world
With love and forgiveness
And a whole lot of wonder.

Finding Jesus in Every Season

Follow author Jane Rubietta on her daily journey through each season of the year to gain perspective, refresh your soul, and continue the journey. Tracing the lives of some of the Bible's greatest characters, these are transformational devotionals that encourage great depth. Walk through these stories from the Bible and experience life as these great characters did, gaining fresh faith and hope for your journey along the way.

A free group leader's guide is available for each devotional at www.wphresources.com.

Finding Your Promise
(spring)
ISBN: 978-0-89827-896-5
eBook: 978-0-89827-897-2

Finding Your Name
(summer)
ISBN: 978-0-89827-898-9
eBook: 978-0-89827-899-6

Finding Your Dream
(fall)
ISBN: 978-0-89827-900-9
eBook: 978-0-89827-901-6

Finding Your Way
(winter)
ISBN: 978-0-89827-894-1
eBook: 978-0-89827-895-8

1.800.493.7539   wphstore.com